Traditional
BRITISH QUILTS

Traditional
BRITISH QUILTS

Dorothy Osler

B.T. Batsford Ltd·London

First published 1987
© Dorothy Osler 1987
All rights reserved. No part of this publication may be reproduced
in any form or by any means without permission from the Publishers

ISBN 0 7134 4760 5

Printed in Great Britain by
Anchor Brendon Ltd
Tiptree, Essex

for the Publishers
B. T. Batsford Ltd
4 Fitzhardinge Street
London W1H 0AH

Contents

Acknowledgement

Much of the information and illustration in this book could not have been brought together without the help of many people. It is with pleasure and gratitude that I acknowledge this.

In Wales my thanks to: Clare Claridge, Kate Lewis and Gwen Luffmann; Ilid Anthony, formerly of the Welsh Folk Museum, St Fagans; Sally Moss of Carmarthen Museum; and Kevin Mason of Brecon Museum. In Scotland, Daisy Aitchison, Mabel Preston, Elizabeth Rosie, Val Stewart and Margaret Swain all helped in individual ways, as did Naomi Tarrant of the National Museums of Scotland, and Veronica Hartwich of Dundee Art Galleries and Museums.

In the West of England, Jeremy Pearson of Exeter City Museum; Valerie Stevens of Somerset County Museum, Taunton; Sheila Betterton of the American Museum, Bath; Kate Brown of Bristol City Museum and Art Gallery (Blaise Castle House); Sue Welsh and Alison Carter of Cheltenham Art Gallery and Museums; and the staff of Hereford County Museum all gave their time to allow access to their collections. To the family of Elizabeth Hake I owe a special debt.

In the North of England my thanks to: Amy Emms MBE, Irene Bell, Florence Fletcher, Belle Shepherd, Mrs Ripley, Mrs Snaith and Mrs Hughes; Rosemary Allan of Beamish Museum; Lorna Hamilton of Carlisle Museum and Art Gallery; Joanna Hashagen of Bowes Museum, Barnard Castle; Clare Rose of the Castle Museum, York; the staff at the Shipley Art Gallery, Gateshead (Tyne and Wear Museum Service), Northumberland Record Office, Tyne and Wear Archives, and Newcastle City Libraries.

I must also thank: Linda Parry of the Victoria and Albert Museum, London; Guy Holborn of Lincoln's Inn Library; and Miss J. A. Elliott of CoSIRA. For logistical help in a variety of ways my thanks to: Anne and Deborah Tuck; Monica Jones; Peter Dickinson of Treen Woodcraft; Beamish Hall Residential College; and Robertsons (Photographers) of Gosforth. I owe a special debt to Frances Williams for so often being the extra pair of hands (and eyes) so necessary when working through collections of quilts. My thanks must also go to my many colleagues and friends in the Quilters' Guild who have helped in a number of ways.

My niece Susan Walker, my daughter Margaret and Mary Robson have all helped to produce the final typescript and I am deeply grateful for their assistance. My husband Adrian and Lucy Morrill have given invaluable help with the illustrations. But to my nearest and dearest I must also say a special 'thank you' for their patience and forbearance during the many hours over the past months when I must have seemed buried, both physically and metaphorically, in quilts.

D.O.
Newcastle upon Tyne, 1986

PHOTOGRAPHIC ACKNOWLEDGEMENTS

I wish to thank the following institutions for permission to reproduce photographs of quilts in their collections: Beamish North of England Open Air Museum for figures 6, 7, 10, 11, 13, 15, 50, 54, 59, 60, 62, 64, 65, and colour plates 3 and 8; Bowes Museum, Barnard Castle, for colour plates 2 and 6; Bristol City Museum and Art Gallery for figures 68 and 72; Carlisle Museum and Art Gallery for figures 49 and 57; Dundee Art Galleries and Museums for figure 89; National Museum of Wales (Welsh Folk Museum, St Fagans) for figures 4, 5, 16, 76, 78, 79, 80, 81, 82, 84 and 88; National Museums of Scotland for figures 48 and 93; Castle Museum, York, for colour plate 1. Figures 42, 43, 46 and 47 are reproduced by permission of the Trustees of the Victoria and Albert Museum, London, as are figures 83, 85 and 86 from the Mavis Fitzrandolph collection.

I am grateful to the following for allowing quilts in their possession to be photographed: Hereford County Museum for figures 8 and 45; Carlisle Museum and Art Gallery for figure 55; Frances Williams for colour plates 4, 5 and 7; Mrs C. Spoors for figure 90; and Mrs M. Webster for figure 92.

For permission to reproduce material in their possession I must thank: Lincoln's Inn Library, London, for figure 44; Northumberland Record Office and the Allgood family for figure 52; Newcastle City Libraries (Local History) for figure 56; Shipley Art Gallery (Tyne and Wear Museum Service), and Amy Emms for figures 66 and 67; Shipley Art Gallery and Mrs Snaith for figure 63; Shipley Art Gallery and Belle Shepherd for figure 61; and the family of Elizabeth Hake for figures 70, 71, 74 and 75.

Introduction

In these times when nearly everything we wear and use must be turned out in millions by machines, it is a refreshing glimpse of beauty to see the work that these women are able to do with their own fingers and their native genius. I am convinced that in the future if our people are to remain balanced, they must develop in crafts and creative work. This is all the more true because I believe that in the future people will tend to have more leisure instead of less.

Margaret Bondfield, Minister of Labour (1930)[1]

With these far-sighted words, Margaret Bondfield opened an exhibition of quilts at the Dorchester Hotel, London, in July 1930. The exhibition displayed the work of quilters from South Wales and Durham for a scheme initiated by the Rural Industries Bureau. It was a significant moment for quiltmaking in Britain for two reasons. Firstly, it created once again a situation whereby quilts were made by one level of society for use by another (higher?) level. And secondly, the quiltmaking tradition in Britain was at last receiving some kind of national acclaim. Alas, it was to be short-lived.

Half a century later it is in a sense these two aspects of quiltmaking which provide something of the rationale for this book. It is – and I stress – a personal view of the *role* of quilts and quiltmaking within British society and an attempt to explain and describe the types of traditional quilts made in Britain (i.e. England, Scotland and Wales) so that the full extent of the British tradition can be better understood. And, for the quilting enthusiast, I shall describe how traditional quilts were made and how they can be made with materials and equipment available today.

First, I should explain what I mean by a 'traditional quilt' and why I am concerned chiefly with these quilts and not the broader theme of quilting *per se*. Quilting can take three main forms: (1) wadded quilting, a sandwich of three fabric layers; (2) cord quilting where cord is inserted between parallel lines of stitching; and (3) stuffed quilting where some kind of filling is pressed into areas of pattern to give them greater relief. All three types were produced in Britain but only one – wadded quilting – significantly entered the lives and homes of the ordinary working people of Britain and so became a part of a traditional way of life. It is these wadded quilts – the quilts of the people 'usually left out of history'[2] which I consider to be the traditional quilts of Britain.

I am, of course, not the first to research and document traditional quilts. In the 1930s, Elizabeth Hake assiduously recorded the quilts she discovered in the West of England. Her book, *English Quilting: Old and New*, was published in 1937. Twenty years later, Mavis Fitzrandolph wrote *Traditional Quilting*, a thoughtful and thorough account of the extensive fieldwork, documentation and organization she had undertaken from the 1920s onwards whilst working for the Rural Industries Bureau. In 1972, Averil Colby produced her more broadly based book *Quilting*.

It is a fact that since Averil Colby's book was published, few traditional British-style quilts have been made. So what is there to add? In the 15 years which have elapsed since then, more attention has been paid to recording the domestic and working lives of the ordinary people of Britain. Various kinds of schemes for recording oral history have been set up and, of these, two have made specific attempts to record what is still remembered of traditional quilting in Britain. Tyne and Wear Museums' Craft Record is now an invaluable source of information on North Country quilting and, though still small, the Quilters' Guild Tape Archive also contains much of significance. These searching interviews with quilters and those who remember the circumstances in which quilts were made bring a new perspective. Traditional quiltmaking needs to be interpreted not just in historical and aesthetic terms, but in relation to social and cultural pressures and constraints. And with this new perspective, new questions arise – questions which go right to the core of the reasons why quilts were made.

The revival of interest in quiltmaking, too, has brought its own demands. The 'quilt revival' began in earnest in the 1970s in Britain, fed largely by contact with the American tradition of patchwork and quilting. But as interest and expertise have grown, quiltmakers want to know more about the British tradition. What types of quilts were made, where, when, why – and how? How did regional styles develop? How do Welsh quilts differ from North Country ones?

With, I hope, a fresh pair of hands and eyes, and my own 'new technology' (cameras and tape recorder), I have travelled not only through my native North-East England, but to Yorkshire, Cumbria, Scotland, Wales, the Welsh Borders and the West of England to see what remains of the quilting tradition in Britain. I have searched through archives, looked through both public and private collections and talked to those for whom quiltmaking – past or present – had or has some significance. I have listened to countless (and amusing) anecdotes and I have tried to assimilate all the evidence – documentary and oral – into some kind of meaningful whole. At times it has seemed a daunting task and I am conscious that, in some respects at least, I have only scratched the surface. But I hope I shall encourage others to dig deeper.

One area presented an immediate problem. Though individual patterns might have specific names, the British quiltmaking tradition has never had any widely accepted terminology for describing quilt types. No simple solution to this problem was apparent. How far should American quilt names be applied to British quilts? Should quilts be described primarily according to their cover design, or to their quilting design? On British quilts, there is not necessarily any direct relationship between the two.

After considerable thought, I eventually attempted what is, I hope, a straightforward classification of quilt types according to both cover design and quilting design. This is fully described in Chapter 2, Traditional Quilt Design, and I have used the terminology throughout the book. I hope my classification, and indeed the whole of the book, will prove of interest and use to those who wish to understand the British quiltmaking tradition. But most of all, I hope it will bring a wider appreciation of the individuals and circumstances which combined to produce what are, arguably, some of the most beautiful vernacular artefacts ever made in Britain.

Note. In accordance with convention, pattern names are in italics throughout the book (except in the figure captions). In the illustrations, the pattern lines drawn around templates, or template shapes, are represented by solid lines; those drawn in freehand are represented by broken lines.

Part One
Making Traditional Quilts

1 Materials and Equipment

The long frames were always to be seen somewhere in our house.

M. Cain (1978)[1]

A traditional wadded quilt is a form of textile sandwich. It has three layers: a top cover, a bottom cover, and the layer in between variously known as the wadding, filling or padding in Britain, and batting in America. The three layers are held together by stitches which have both a practical and decorative purpose. They hold the layers firmly together but the stitches also create a low-relief pattern and soft texture which decorates an otherwise flat layer of fabric and creates an almost sculptured appearance.

In the following sections the basic materials and equipment needed for quilting, and the choices available to the quiltmaker today, will be described. At the same time, it seems appropriate to indicate briefly, at this point, how the materials and equipment used for traditional quilts have changed over the years. Fashion, availability, cost and traditional use are all important factors affecting choice, particularly of materials, and their influence on this traditional craft cannot be ignored.

FABRICS

Before choosing fabric for the top and bottom covers of a quilt, a few practical points should be considered. Is the quilt to be reversible? If so, fabrics of a suitable quality should be chosen for *both* covers. Is the quilt to be washed rather than dry-cleaned? If so, fabrics must be suitable for domestic washing and be colourfast. Where is the quilt to be used? If it is to fit into a particular room-setting then the colours and fabric type should be chosen with this in mind. How durable is the quilt to be? The fabrics and thread should be able to withstand the ravages of time and wear if it is to survive as a family 'treasure'.

Fabrics for a wadded quilt should be closely woven, to prevent the fibres of the wadding working through, and smooth; fabrics with a nap, such as velvet, do not show quilting patterns to best effect. Fabrics should also be soft and fine enough for a needle to penetrate easily. Some quiltmakers prefer fabrics with a glazed finish because the light reflection from the shiny surface has a particular effect on the low-relief surface of a quilt; but the glazed finish on some fabrics will not survive much domestic laundering.

Household inventories from the sixteenth century onwards tell us something of the type of material used for quilts in the past. Most sixteenth- and seventeenth-century quilts were of expensive and much-prized fabrics such as silk, sarsenet (a soft silk material), satin and taffeta, though more hard-wearing fabrics such as fustian (a type of cotton fabric) and holland (a fine bleached linen) are also recorded. The seventeenth century saw the arrival of imported Indian cottons, both as ready-made quilts and as painted fabric lengths quilted in England and sold as fashionable bed covers, amongst other uses. It is not until the late seventeenth century that any firm evidence appears of the use of less expensive woollen fabrics, like serge, or even of homespun, like linsey-woolsey, for quilts. Linen remained fashionable in the eighteenth century, especially for corded quilts, as did silk.

The Industrial Revolution led to a rapid expansion in the manufacture and printing of cotton fabrics after about 1760. Technical advances in spinning, weaving, printing and, later, dyeing, led to inexpensive cotton fabrics becoming readily available. Their impact on quiltmaking was as important as on other areas of textile use. Silk, satin and linen declined in popularity and cotton quilts, especially patchwork ones, were widely made from the mid eighteenth century through to the twentieth century. But alongside these cotton ones, quilts of warmer homespun materials, like wool or linsey-woolsey, continued to be made, their function more utilitarian than decorative.

The second half of the nineteenth century saw the increased and widespread use of a variety of new cotton fabrics. The invention and rapid adoption of chemical dyes, after 1856, led to the availability of inexpensive colourfast cottons. Advances in printing and finishing processes helped make other fabrics, such as cotton sateen, available and cheap.

As fabrics became less expensive, so there was less need for economy: many quilts were made with bought materials which led to the decline of patchwork quilts and an increase in the number of wholecloth and strippy quilts made. This trend continued right up to the late 1920s when, under the influence of the Rural Industries Bureau, silk and satin quilts were once again produced – this time for the 'up-market' London galleries. Sateen, crêpe de chine and poplin quilts were also made by these RIB quilters and these, too, found a ready market in London. But these changes were short-lived, for rationing of fabrics in the Second World War put an end to the RIB scheme and, indeed, almost put an end to traditional quilting in Britain.

The quiltmaker today can choose from a variety of natural and man-made fibres. Of the natural fibres, cotton fabrics are an ever-popular choice: they are durable, easy to handle, and available in a wide variety of patterns and colours, though a wide range of solid-colour fabrics is usually available only from specialist suppliers. Silk and satin are also easy to obtain and glazed furnishing cotton, similar to cotton sateen, is becoming more readily available. Wool fabrics are less popular because, unless very fine, they are difficult to quilt easily; linen of a suitable quality is very hard to find.

Synthetic fibres of various kinds and synthetic/natural-fibre mixes are widely available. They are popular with dressmakers because of their easy-care and hard-wearing properties but quiltmakers are, on the whole, less enthusiastic. Synthetic fibres can be harsh and less pliable than natural ones but some mixed-fibre fabrics, like polyester-cotton (either glazed or unglazed), can be suitable, provided the polyester content is not too high, as can the polyester forms of satin and crêpe de chine.

The growth of interest in both patchwork and quilting in recent years, and the consequent demand for suitable, good-quality fabrics, has led to the establishment of a number of specialist suppliers throughout Britain, as in the other parts of the world which the 'quilt revival' has reached. They all supply a wide range, mainly of pure cotton fabrics in a variety of prints and solid colours, usually on a mail-order basis. A list of (current) suppliers is given on page 165. An even greater variety of fabrics is available in North America: many of these have been specially printed, from commissioned designs or from old blocks, specifically for the quilting market.

WADDING

The layer of wadding in a quilt can have two functions: (1) to provide warmth; and (2) to rise up between the lines of stitching, so emphasizing the quilted pattern and creating the relief and texture characteristic of this craft. Of these two functions, one is utilitarian and the other decorative but which is the prime function varies from quilt to quilt. Some cotton quilts have such a thin padding that they must have been made chiefly as decorative bed furnishings, whereas thickly padded quilts were clearly intended for warmth, if not for decoration.

The earliest recorded, and the earliest surviving, examples of wadded quilts known to have been made in Britain were mostly filled with wool, readily available from local flocks. Cotton, however, had been imported into Britain from early in the fifteenth century[2] and its use as a filling was both recognized and recommended. 'I do advertise you', wrote Andrew Boorde (1542) in his *Compendyous Regyment or a Dietary of helth*,[3] 'to cause to be made a good thick quilt of cotton, or else of pure flocks or of clean wool, and let the covering of it be of white fustian, and lay it on the featherbed that you do lie on; and in your bed lie not too hot nor too cold, but in a temperance.' But imported cotton was no doubt expensive and probably only rarely used.

It was not until the nineteenth century that cotton wool suitable for a filling was manufactured in Britain. It was first produced 'between 1820 and 1830 . . . in the Manchester district, of cotton wool from cotton of shorter staple than that used for spinning'.[4] Prior to this, most of the quilts with a cotton filling in use in Britain were those imported from India; even the painted chintzes imported then quilted in England had a wool filling.

By the mid-nineteenth century, however, cotton had clearly replaced wool wadding in the North of England, but in Wales and South-West England cotton never became so extensively used. Why should this be so? It could be that choice was governed, in the regions of Britain, by availability. Quilters in the North of England were closer to the areas of manufacture of cotton wool and, once demand was firmly established, local shops kept a plentiful supply in the areas where quilters were most active. It could equally be that in areas other than the North quilters simply preferred the quality of a wool filling.

There are few records before this period, but it would appear that the nineteenth century also saw the introduction of blanket fillings. Blankets were used as wadding in all types of quilts in all regions but 'everyday' quilts in particular were likely to be filled with a blanket. Economy was very much a feature of these 'everyday' quilts, with covers pieced either from scraps or from inexpensive cottons. And not only blankets were used: flannelette sheets, old woollen garments, even old net curtains can be found inside what can almost be regarded as 'textile middens'. Welsh 'everyday' quilts, in particular, could be very thick and heavy from several layers of filling of various kinds. No doubt they served their purpose!

The patterns of usage established in the nineteenth century carried through well into the twentieth century, in the regions of Britain where quilting survived. But when the Rural Industries Bureau established its quilting scheme in the late 1920s and 1930s (see pages 100–102), it provided wool for wadding even to the quilters in County Durham, where cotton had been in use for several generations. This indicates a deliberate preference for the qualities of wool in their 'luxury' quilts.

Sheep's or lambs' wool, cotton wool or an old blanket were the common types of wadding used in traditional quilts up until the Second World War. Since then, polyester waddings have added to the choice. Domette has been used but only rarely. Mention has also been made[5] of the use of thistledown, but Mavis Fitzrandolph scornfully dismisses this with the following:

One reads in articles on quilting that thistledown was used as padding. I have never heard of this from any *quilter*, but I was told by someone who was intrigued by the idea, and started to collect thistledown, that after she had assiduously gathered it throughout one summer she had a bagful of dry material which was heavy though it had shrunk to small bulk, and had no fluffiness or resilience. Thistledown in fact is a quite different sort of substance from cotton wool and I doubt whether it was ever used to pad quilts.[6]

With the choice of wadding now available to the quiltmaker, which is best to use? The answer is not a straightforward one: each type has its own physical properties and gives a different tactile quality to a quilt. The fabrics of the covers will influence the choice: polyester wadding is quite suitable, for example, with cotton and polyester-cotton covers, but a softer, natural-fibre wadding might be more suitable for a fine, soft, silk fabric. The quilting design is also an important factor: cotton and wool wadding must be closely quilted to prevent the fibres bunching up when the quilt is washed, but polyester wadding is more stable and does not require such close quilting. Practical considerations are also important. Can the wadding be bought ready to use or will much preparation be required? How will it wash and dry? How expensive is it?

With these aspects in mind, choose from the following:

Polyester   Polyester wadding (sold under the trade names Terylene in Britain and Dacron in America) is available in a variety of thicknesses and qualities. This type of man-made wadding is now much used: it is cheap, light, easy to use, and washes and dries well. Polyester wadding is also the only type available in full bed-size widths. It is suitable for all types of quilt but especially for patchwork and appliquéd quilts where close quilting is not an integral part of the design.

Polyester fillings do, however, have a harsher quality than the softer fibres of cotton and wool and, like wool, they can suffer from the problem of 'bearding', where the fibres of the wadding work through the fabric of the covers. To overcome this, some polyester waddings are bonded. Alternatively, a layer of muslin can be used between the wadding and the fabric cover.

If you plan to use a polyester wadding, choose a thickness and quality suitable for the purpose of the quilt. Do not choose the inferior, thin and loosely matted wadding available from some department stores – it will leave a quilt looking very flat. Specialist suppliers have a wider range of better-quality wadding available. For fine hand quilting, a 2 oz thickness is usually recommended: with a thicker wadding it is difficult to keep the stitches small.

Cotton   Cotton-wool wadding was originally sold in pound packets. Though still commercially available, it is now sold by length and comes enclosed in a papery 'skin'. It is still a good-quality wadding, but now comparatively expensive.

Cotton wool is less springy than sheep's or lambs' wool, though it is still soft and warm. However, when washed, cotton wool tends to bunch up into lumps so, if using a cotton wadding, no area more than 4 × 4 cm ($1\frac{1}{2}$ × $1\frac{1}{2}$ in.) should be left unquilted.

Wool   Wool from the fleece, particularly lambs' wool, makes an excellent filling. It is warm, yet soft and light, and retains its springiness even when washed. The great disadvantage is that it must first be prepared – a lengthy operation. It is not easily available in a ready-to-use state. However, for the quiltmaker who wishes to prepare and use a wool filling, instructions are given on page 66.

As with polyester wadding, 'bearding' can also be a problem with wool. The traditional solution, and one still used, is to put a layer of muslin between the wadding and the cover.

Whatever wadding is chosen, it will affect the visual and tactile quality of a finished quilt. Since it is hard adequately to describe these, I would advise the would-be quiltmaker to try some small samples of quilting, with different types of wadding, to see at first hand and better judge the choice of wadding to use.

FRAMES AND HOOPS

When hand quilting, some means of keeping the three layers of fabric evenly together, and under some tension, is generally agreed to be essential. The quilting frame has long served this purpose and, in recent years, quilting hoops have been introduced to perform the same function. It is possible to quilt without a frame or hoop (known as lap-quilting) but, even with small items, there is always the possibility that the layers may move on each other and the work become puckered. Quilters, past and present, are emphatic about the need for a hoop or frame.

The traditional quilting frame was used throughout Britain, in much the same basic form. Simple in construction and easy to make at home, its main parts are shown in fig. 1. It has two long wooden bars, known as rails or runners (*a*), and two shorter thinner wooden pieces which slot into the rails. These shorter pieces are called stretchers (*b*) because they are used to tension the quilt in the frame, but they were also known as swords in the West of England.[7] Each rail is usually made from a square- or rectangular-sectioned timber with a slot (*c*) cut at each end in the side section to accommodate the stretcher ends. The slot should be big enough to allow the stretcher to slide easily through but not so big that the stretcher can move freely inside the slot. A length of webbing (*d*), long enough to attach to the full width of a quilt, is tacked or nailed to the inner edge of the rail. 'Be sure to use brass tacks', I was told by one elderly quilter in Northumberland, 'or you might get rust marks on your quilt if it stays in the frame over the winter.'[8]

The length of the rails has to be sufficient to include the webbing, stretcher slots and enough at each rail end (*e*) to rest on whatever support is being used for the frame. It follows that, for a double-bed sized quilt, the rails need to be 2.4–2.7 m (8–9 ft) long. Smaller items can be quilted in a large frame if an extra set of slots (*f*) is cut inside the outer set, but smaller frames were made (and still are) for quilting cot quilts, cushion covers and other small pieces.

1. Traditional quilt frame

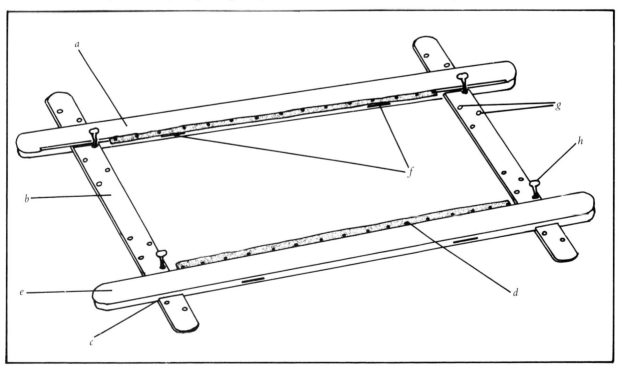

*2. Contemporary quilt
frame*

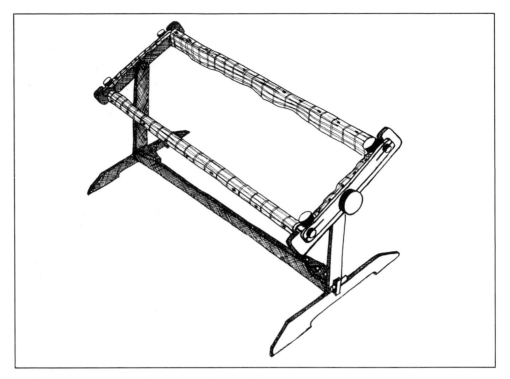

The stretchers are made from timber with a thinner section – 8 × 1 cm (3 × $\frac{3}{8}$ in.) is adequate. They are also much shorter than the rails (only about 1 m (39 in.) for the largest frames) and are drilled with holes to take the pegs which keep the frame positioned in its rectangular shape. There are usually two rows of holes, 2–2.5 cm ($\frac{3}{4}$–1 in.) apart, and drilled alternately (*g*), though some frames have only one row. The pegs (*h*) which fit into the holes are usually tapered wooden ones, home-made and often very crude, although a variety of metal pegs or clamps can be adapted to serve the purpose.

Quilt frames can be made from either hard or soft timber, though softwood will produce a lighter frame. Timbers must be carefully sanded to a smooth finish to prevent the fabric of the quilt catching. The two ends which come into direct contact with the fabric (the rails) can be covered with a fine, clean cotton or similar fabric to help keep the quilt clean. The ends of the timbers can be left as square or rectangular sections but they can, if wished, be rounded to remove the sharp corners. The ends of the stretchers, in particular, were often rounded to make it easier to fit them into the slots of the rails.

Some local adaptations were made to the traditional frame. In the Allendale district of Northumberland, round rails were commonly used because they did not mark the fabric as it was rolled.[9] Just south of Allendale, frames with a ratchet system for rolling have been recorded in Weardale.[10] I have also been told that frames were sometimes attached to pulleys in the ceiling so they could be hoisted out of the way when not in use – a system akin to the once ubiquitous clothes-dryer.

Traditional quilt frames were never bought from a shop. Those that have survived were passed on through the generations and many were probably originally made, as the need arose, by a male relative or friend of the quilter. Others were made, as Elizabeth Hake records,[11] by the village carpenter for a few shillings.

As a simple basic frame – easy to make, easy to use and easy to store in minimal space when not in use – the traditional quilt frame has much to commend it. It differs little from the basic embroidery frame known to have been used for centuries and adapted for other textile crafts, like lace-making and mat-making, as well as quilting. It usually had no stand, but was supported at either end, either on a table or chest top or on the backs of chairs. Some quilters, however, did have trestles on which they could rest their frames.

Quiltmakers today can purchase ready-made frames in a variety of sizes from table-top size to king-size, with or without stands. In quality and finish they are undoubtedly superior to the traditional frame, with improvements such as round rails and rolling mechanisms; some even have a pivoting top (fig. 2) so that the work can be angled (helps the back-ache problem!). As a tool for holding the quilt layers together whilst quilting, a frame which takes the full width of a quilt is preferable. But the disadvantage of a large frame is the amount of room-space it occupies and its lack of portability.

The quilting hoop is smaller and more portable. Basically a sturdy form of embroidery hoop, the layers are secured and tensioned by means of a screw-fitting on the outer hoops. It is possible to quilt in an armchair with a hoop tilted to whatever angle is convenient for stitching (fig. 3). Hoops come in a variety of sizes from 25 cm (10 in.) diameter to 58 cm (23

3. Quilting in a hoop

in.) diameter; some are available on stands with a pivot to adjust the angle. Oval as well as circular hoops are available, but these are not a wise choice because the fabric is not evenly tensioned in an oval frame.

Inevitably, the convenience of the hoop has to be weighed against its disadvantages. More careful preparation of the layers of the quilt is required before it is placed in the hoop for quilting (see page 73) and it is possible for some fabrics to become permanently crushed or marked where held in the hoop. A quilting hoop should *never* be left fixed on a piece of quilting when it is not being worked on.

NEEDLES AND THIMBLES

The usual choice of needle for hand quilting is a between needle (a short, small-eyed one), usually size 8, 9 or 10. Longer needles are likely to bend too much with the rocking motion needed to produce a line of running stitches. The size of between is a matter of personal preference; I usually use a size 10. The larger size (8) can be bought in local haberdashers, but the smaller sizes (9 and 10) are normally obtainable only from specialist suppliers.

Though always a popular choice, it seems unlikely that a between-type needle was invariably used by traditional quilters in the past. Older informants, particularly those who only quilted for their own needs, can be quite vague about the type of needle used either by themselves or their predecessors. When I was talking to one Welsh quilter, she opened a piece of unfinished quilting, stored away since the 1930s, to reveal a long sharps needle still threaded with the thread to the last line of stitches!

A well-fitting thimble for the middle finger of the sewing hand is essential. This finger controls the needle, pushes it through the layers of fabric and produces the rocking motion required to take several stitches together. Thimbles can also be worn on the finger of the hand under the work used to feel the needle coming through, and on the thumb of the quilting hand. If some protection is not given to these fingers, they will become sore from pricking. I now wear a metal thimble, hammered flat at the end, on the middle finger of the hand below the work, as advocated by Michael James, the American quilt artist. Another solution is to wear a finger cut from an old leather glove. However, some quiltmakers prefer not to protect these fingers, so that they can feel the needle better. The traditional quilters' solution to this problem was to rub surgical spirit into the finger ends to harden them.

THREAD

The thread used to stitch the layers of a quilt together, and so form the quilting pattern, must be strong enough to serve its purpose and to survive intact through use and laundering.

All the natural-fibre threads – silk, linen and cotton – have been used on traditional quilts and have survived well. Even on worn quilts, the stitching seems to give way only when the covers themselves show excessive signs of wear. Threads were chosen with some care for all except the most 'everyday' quilts. Seventeenth- and eighteenth-century silk and satin quilts were quilted with silk thread, usually in a colour to match the top cover. Linen quilts could be sewn in either a cotton or a linen thread but, in the seventeenth and eighteenth centuries, there was clearly a vogue for quilting, even on linen, with yellow silk.

On nineteenth- and early twentieth-century 'everyday' quilts a coarse thread, usually a tough linen one, was used, white or off-white on light-coloured covers, but a darker tone on quilts like the Welsh wool ones. On 'best' quilts, a finer thread chosen to blend with the fabrics of the covers was used. On late nineteenth- and twentieth-century quilts, a coarse (No. 40) cotton thread, or a glazed cotton one, was the usual choice. Silk threads, however, continued to be used on silk or satin quilts. After the Second World War, surviving traditional quilters continued to use cotton thread although, by now, finer dressmaking threads were equally popular. The relatively new polyester threads, again of dressmaking quality, have also been used in recent years, though I would not recommend them.

Waxing thread was not a common practice amongst traditional quilters in the North of England, but Welsh quilters did wax thread to ease its passage through wool wadding. Though not essential, running thread through beeswax before quilting does strengthen it and prevent tangling.

Specialist suppliers and haberdashers now provide the quiltmaker with a variety of threads, in a range of colours. Use silk thread for a silk or satin quilt; for most other quilts one of the 100 per cent cotton threads will be suitable. Specially manufactured quilting thread is now widely available from both specialist suppliers and some department stores, but a No. 40 cotton thread or fine crochet cotton can substitute. Linen thread can also be used but it is available in only a limited colour range.

TEMPLATES

Templates are required for some of the pattern outlines. They can be bought or made from a variety of materials. Those purchased from specialist suppliers are generally of clear plastic and in stencil form, with the internal filling lines cut out so they can be drawn in. Home-made templates are simple outlines and any internal filling needs to be drawn in by hand. Thick card was most often used, but plywood, plastic or even sheet metal can be used if particularly durable templates are required. In areas where the tradition of quilting was particularly strong, such as the North Pennine Dales, templates would be carefully preserved and handed on through generations.

It is worth acquiring and carefully keeping a good stock of templates. Some organizations (see page 165) sell paper sheets printed with pattern outlines. These can be cut out and mounted on to card. Surviving traditional quilters, or the relatives of those who have gone, are usually willing to allow copies to be made of their templates. Patterns for templates can also be copied from surviving or illustrated quilts. Quiltmakers can, of course, devise their own pattern templates; in the past, new patterns could be closely and jealously guarded within a family.

MEASURING TOOLS

When the design of a quilting pattern is worked out, measuring equipment is usually needed to mark out critical areas like the border widths and the pattern repeat along a border edge, and to mark some infill patterns. Long rulers (metre or yard sticks) are particularly useful and a T-square helps to align border angles correctly. Also useful are 'quilter's quarters' – perspex rods of varying widths which can be used for drawing infill patterns.

PATTERN MARKERS

Some kind of marker is needed to draw out the quilting design on one of the fabric covers. Ideally, a clear thin line should be produced that is easily visible when quilting but removable or invisible when the work is completed.

The traditional quilters of the past had few choices available. Chalk (tailor's chalk or even blackboard chalk) was commonly used in Wales where marking was done with the quilt already in the frame. In the North of England, where the quilt design was often marked out before the quilt was put in the frame, chalk was less popular because the marks rubbed off too easily as work proceeded. Some North Country quilters preferred to needle-mark – to draw around the templates with a yarn needle, leaving a clear impression on the cover.

The quilt designers of Allendale and Weardale (see pages 117–21), however, preferred to draw out their designs with a blue (or occasionally yellow) pencil. They needed a mark which would last through packaging, posting, even peddling, until it reached its eventual customer. And then it had to last through quilting!

The quiltmaker today can choose from a variety of markers, but no single one is ideal for all purposes. Assess your needs and choose from the following:

Dressmaker's chalk pencils   Readily available in several colours, these pencils, unlike slab tailor's chalk, can be kept sharpened to a fine point. The marks do rub off easily, so the pencils are unsuitable for hoop quilting, or if the design has to be marked before the quilt is set in a frame. Once the design is quilted, however, the chalk lines are easy to erase.

Chinagraph pencils   Available in a variety of colours, these pencils leave a bold clear line which lasts through constant handling (useful for hoop quilting). The lines, however, are difficult to remove – two, sometimes three, washes are needed before they have disappeared.

Coloured pencils   If a coloured pencil in a shade slightly darker than the fabric cover is used, and the lines are drawn lightly, they show up well enough to follow when quilting but disappear or brush away when the work is complete. Alternatively, a water-soluble coloured pencil (available from artist's suppliers) in a clearly visible colour can be used and the lines sponged away when quilting is completed.

Dressmaker's carbon   Available in yellow and blue, dressmaker's carbon is useful for transferring paper patterns, rather than card templates, on to a fabric cover. The pattern is pinned on to the carbon and the lines are traced with a pencil or tracing wheel. The marks will only disappear, however, with washing.

Yarn needle   A yarn needle or similar pointed tool (rug needle or bradawl) was used by many North Country quilters. In practice, it is not suitable on all types of fabrics and errors in marking can be difficult to remove. It is particularly suitable for fabrics with a sheen, on which the needle marks show clearly when quilting, but disappear once the work is completed.

2 Traditional Quilt Design

Knowledge which is handed down by word of mouth is bound to undergo some change from generation to generation and there will be many streams of it.

Mavis Fitzrandolph (1954)[1]

'Design' and 'pattern' are two words often confused and used to mean much the same thing. Let me begin by defining what I mean by these terms and how I intend to use them. The *design* of a traditional quilt is the overall arrangement, or plan, of the individual *patterns* used. In a sense, by using these terms in this way, I am departing from traditional terminology and superimposing a contemporary one on a traditional craft. A traditional quilter would never have used the word design but would always have spoken of *pattern* in a rather loose way to mean either an individual pattern unit such as a *rose* or *feather*, or the overall arrangement of the patterns. But in the interests of clarity and further discussion I feel it worth making the distinction clear.

The design of a traditional quilt can have two parts: (1) the design of the covers of the quilt; and (2) the design of the quilting itself. On some quilts, the quilting design will be planned to relate to the design of one of the covers (usually the one intended as the top cover) but it is a feature of some British quilts that the quilting design does not have any direct relationship to the cover design (for example the quilts in colour plates 3 and 4). By contrast the quilt illustrated in colour plate 10 shows a clear relationship between the quilting design and the *star* patchwork of the cover.

Because the quilting design and the cover design on traditional British quilts do not always have a direct relationship, it becomes necessary to consider them separately. I do not, however, wish to follow what has, to a large extent, been previous practice: to ignore the designs of the quilt covers and concentrate only on the quilting design. I feel this has led to a distorted impression of the types of traditional quilts produced in Britain and understated the part patchwork and appliqué have played in the tradition. Wholecloth quilts (made from a single fabric), on which the visual interest is created solely by the quilting design, have long been the great strength of British quilting but many beautiful patchwork, appliqué and strippy quilts have been made alongside the wholecloth ones.

I will therefore begin by looking at the traditional designs used for the two sides of a quilt – the covers. They must come first, at least in the order of making a quilt. Except for wholecloth quilts, the cover design is the most visually striking, so that quilts tend to be described initially by the nature of the covers: strippy quilts, medallion quilts, basket quilts, for example, are all familiar and well-understood terms amongst quiltmakers and quilt enthusiasts today.

COVER DESIGNS

The fabric used for the covers of a quilt, and the manner in which they are put together, represent the cover design. The two covers of the same quilt may, however, be of different designs: one side may be a wholecloth cover, whilst the other may be a patchwork, appliqué or strippy one. With some quilts it is clear which side was intended by the maker to be the 'best' side or quilt top. American quilts usually have a distinct 'top' and backing but traditional British quilts were often intended to be reversible in which case neither side was regarded as the 'top' or 'bottom'. On other quilts, a scrap-patchwork cover (which might now be treasured for its charm and simplicity) may have been made for the 'bottom' of a quilt. Such utility scrap-patchwork covers can be found on the undersides of carefully worked strippy and wholecloth quilts.

The cover designs on traditional British quilts show certain common elements, indicating that particular patterns and design plans were worked at different times, throughout Britain. It can be argued, however, that taken as a whole the cover designs of traditional British quilts do not have the strength of the quilting designs. Certainly on some quilts the quality of the cover design is not exceptional, with inaccurate piecing of patchwork shapes or a poorly planned appliqué design. But, equally, in some parts of Britain, cover designs of charm and real quality were produced – their relative simplicity so often their strength.

From the late nineteenth century onwards, though, traditional British quilters have shown a clear preference for wholecloth and strippy covers, no doubt because they provide a plainer surface on which to work elaborate quilting designs, and because these covers are easy to prepare. Only in the recent 'quilt revival' has attention refocused on the traditional patchwork designs of Britain.

Wholecloth covers

Wholecloth covers are made in a single fabric. When both covers of a quilt are wholecloth ones, the quilt may be reversible, with fabrics of a suitable quality (perhaps in different colours) chosen for the two sides. Cot quilts, for example, were sometimes made with a blue fabric for one cover and pink for the other – it shouldn't stretch the imagination too far to guess the reason for that!

Because so many traditional quilts made in the last hundred years have been wholecloth ones, they have come to be regarded as the classic British quilt 'type'. They are certainly one of the oldest types of wadded quilt, dating back at least to the seventeenth century, though fabrics and colours have varied through the centuries according to fashion, availability and cost.

The wholecloth surface is ideal for showing a quilting design to good effect if a solid-colour fabric rather than a printed one is chosen. No other surface pattern then competes for attention. At the same time, any deficiencies of design or workmanship will clearly show so the quilting design must be carefully planned – and executed – to ensure that all the pattern elements have a balanced and harmonious relationship. All the various types of quilting designs can be worked on to wholecloth covers although, in practice, 'best' quilts were quilted in a *bordered* design as in figs 4 and 5. Those of a more utilitarian nature, particularly the 'everyday' quilts made in the late nineteenth/early twentieth century, were likely to be quilted in *strip* or *allover* designs. It was not unusual for 'everyday' quilts to be wholecloth ones and to be made from bought fabrics. Cotton fabrics, particularly, were inexpensive; in 1900 cotton fabric could be bought for as little as $2\frac{1}{2}$d ($1\frac{1}{2}$p) a yard,[2] though 6d ($2\frac{1}{2}$p) a yard was an average price: even as late as 1965 cotton sateen could be bought for as little as 2s 11d (about 15p) a yard.

Patterned fabrics have also been used for wholecloth covers: the painted Indian chintzes imported from the seventeenth century onwards were made into quilts amongst other things and simply quilted with *allover* designs (see fig. 45). Floral furnishing chintzes and paisley prints were popular in the earlier part of the twentieth century and were well quilted in a variety of designs. But they were not the best choice for elaborate work; 'flowered material didn't show the work that was put into it'.[3]

A solid-colour fabric is undoubtedly a better choice for a wholecloth cover, and a good-quality fabric should always be chosen. Various types of fabrics with a glazed finish have come in and out of fashion for wholecloth quilts, for example Shantung silk, satin, taffeta, cotton sateen and mercerized cotton poplin. Some of these are still easy to obtain.

Glazed fabrics have not, however, always been in vogue. Unglazed flat and twill weave cottons were used for many nineteenth-century wholecloth covers, particularly on all-white 'best' quilts. Linen too was used but either ceased to be fashionable or became difficult or expensive to buy after about 1850. Wool fabrics (sometimes homespun) were used, particularly in Wales, though they are more difficult to quilt through.

The choice of fabric for a wholecloth cover is, to a large extent, a personal one. Provided that a suitable type of fabric is chosen, i.e. one which is closely woven but easy to stitch through, the colour and finish can be chosen according to taste and eventual use.

4. Wholecloth quilt in cotton with frill made by Miss Mary Williams, Hendre Hall Farm, St Mellons, Gwent: late nineteenth century (244 × 224 cm—96 × 88 in.)

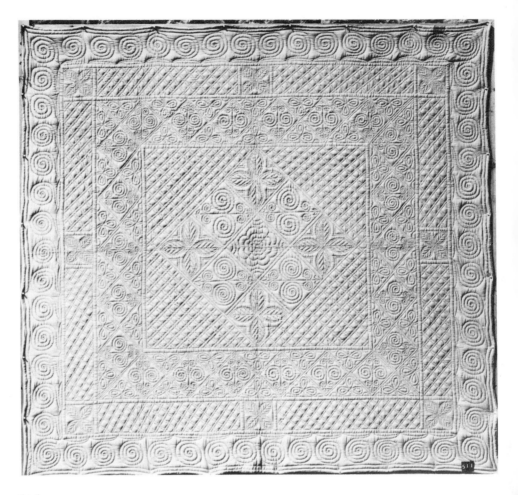

5. *Wholecloth quilt in cotton poplin made in 1933 by Porth quilting group, Rhondda, Glamorgan (188 × 178 cm—74 × 67 in.)*

Strippy covers

Strippy covers – so-called from the colloquial term used to describe them in North-East England – are pieced from fabric strips long enough to run the full length of the quilt. In theory, these fabric strips can be any chosen width but, in practice, traditional strippy covers are usually of strips 23 cm (9 in.) to 30 cm (12 in.) wide.

The oldest strippy quilt so far recorded is a woollen one, in crimson and black, made in the Isle of Man around 1840.[4] How far the strippy quilt pre-dates this period is impossible to say, for no other certain examples of this 'everyday' quilt design are known to have survived from the first half of the nineteenth century. Most surviving strippy quilts have come from the period 1860–1930 when they were made in profusion in the counties of Northumberland and Durham. They were made both by individual quilters for their own use and by the women who ran quilt clubs. Strippy quilts were not, however, unique to North-East England: they were common in the Yorkshire Dales and in Wales and the West of England. But the most attractive and carefully worked examples have come from those most northern counties of England, and were pieced either from bought fabric or from 'the narrow strips which were cut off the edges when the [wholecloth] quilt was finished . . . kept and stitched together and quilted for their own use'.[5]

The cover for a strippy quilt is pieced from an odd number of strips (usually five, seven or

6. Strippy quilt in red and white cottons; North Country: c.1880 (227 × 173 cm—89 × 68 in.)

nine), so one strip is in a central position down the length (fig. 6 and colour plates 7 and 8). Surviving strippy covers are usually pieced by machine and it was, I believe, the ease with which strippy covers could be sewn by machine which led to their profusion once sewing machines became commonplace in homes. Most strippy covers were made in two contrasting fabrics but 'scrap' strippies were also made by piecing lengths of several different fabrics together. 'When I was young I often slept under a quilt stripped red, green and purple', one lady from County Durham remembers.[6]

A strippy cover was usually quilted with a *strip* quilting design (see pages 39–40) with patterns worked down the lengths of the strips. But if a strippy cover was intended for the reverse side of a wholecloth or patchwork quilt (appliqué quilts were never backed with strippy covers) the quilting design could be a *bordered* or an *allover* one.

Any type of fabric suitable for quilting can, in theory, be used for a strippy quilt. Traditionally, though, they were made in inexpensive cotton fabrics reflecting both their status as 'everyday' quilts and their association with a lower social order. Dress cottons (in small floral and sprigged prints or solid colours), tougher twill-weave cotton, and cotton sateen (in solid colours, paisley and floral prints) were all widely used. A popular combination was to alternate plain white calico with a patterned or coloured cotton: Turkey red and white was especially popular but pink, green, yellow and blue fabrics were all commonly combined with white. 'Two Victorian quilts belonging to grandmother . . . were both stripped on one side, one red and white, the other yellow and white with a plain white reverse side' remembers a lady from Northumberland.[7]

Strippy quilts – with a strippy cover and quilted in a *strip* design – are amongst the simplest of traditional quilts to plan and to make. Perhaps this accounts for their enormous popularity in North-East England in the years between 1860 and 1930, when thousands of them must have been made. Many were rough and ready quilts whose function was strictly utilitarian. But when skilfully worked in carefully chosen fabrics they have unique charm and character.

Patchwork covers

A patchwork cover is one which is made from an arrangement of fabric pieces. Patchwork quilts are also referred to as *pieced* quilts, and the way in which the fabric shapes are sewn together is known as *piecing*.

Patchwork covers are made up from one or more patchwork patterns combined in a variety of ways. It is not the purpose of this book to describe in detail the many and varied types of patchwork patterns – these are well described elsewhere – but it is necessary, at this point, to set the patchwork tradition in Britain into some kind of context in order to explain its use in traditional quilts.

The crafts of patchwork and quilting have distinct histories in Britain but they also have a close association first seen in the famous Levens Hall quilt, said to have been made in 1708.[8] The careful arrangement of cruciform, octagon and long hexagon shapes (not the simplest of shapes to combine) suggests a craft already well established. It may be that patchwork in Britain owes its origins to the desire to make the most of fashionable Indian chintzes, first imported in the seventeenth century and used in the Levens Hall quilt, but evidence of organized patchwork in Europe dates right back to medieval times and the close cultural connection between England and the continent of Europe cannot be ignored.

The surviving examples of British patchwork, most of which date from the second half of the eighteenth century onwards, show two clear strands associated with social divisions in British society. On the one hand, multicoloured patchworks of silks, satins, and velvets as well as cottons were pieced in mosaics of diamonds, hexagons and a variety of block patterns. They were worked by the ladies of the upper and middle classes, using the technique now known as 'English paper patchwork', but under the influence of 'bourgeois culture' this style of patchwork gradually filtered down the social scale. In Victorian Britain, such patchwork was ubiquitous, but only occasionally quilted.

In the years between the second half of the eighteenth century and 1900 a simpler but distinctive type of patchwork was combined with quilting to make bed quilts. Its origin is obscure but eventually it found its way into farms and cottages and became firmly established in those parts of Britain remote from metropolitan influence. Using the less expensive cotton fabrics now manufactured and printed in England, or homespun, simple shapes like squares and triangles were pieced with a running stitch rather than the oversewn stitching of 'paper patchwork', to produce medallion and strip patchwork quilts; the oversewn 'paper patchwork' method was still used for some block and mosaic quilts. From 1860 onwards, machine stitching was not infrequently used to replace the previously hand-sewn running stitch. These patchwork covers were well quilted in the quilting designs and styles used in wholecloth quilts.

This 'cottage' type of quilted patchwork can be divided into a small number of well-recognized frameworks or designs. They represent a collective wisdom of patchwork design passed on through generations but precisely how these patterns were described between the generations is unknown. For only the quilts themselves have survived – pattern names, if any, and the customs, practices and symbolism associated with British patchwork quilts have been lost – and the nomenclature now used has come largely from the American tradition. The research and fieldwork done on traditional quilting in Britain, particularly by Elizabeth Hake and Mavis Fitzrandolph, came too late to record much of this patchwork tradition.

Medallion designs   Medallion patchwork designs have a centrepiece (the medallion) surrounded by a series of borders. The central medallion can be either a single large fabric shape, or a patchwork, appliquéd or embroidered block. At one period (the early nineteenth

7. Medallion quilt in multicoloured cottons; North Country: c.1880 (236 × 229 cm—93 × 90 in.)

8. *Medallion quilt in multicoloured cottons and linen with appliquéd centre; West Country: early nineteenth century (223 × 214 cm—88 × 84 in.)*

century) special block-printed chintz panels, produced for general furnishing purposes, were used for the centres of medallion quilts (see fig. 49).

The borders around the central medallion can vary in number but there are always at least two: they usually increase in width towards the edge of the quilt and can be either pieced or in a single fabric. Borders can be square cut at the edges, or squares and rectangles can be set at the corners of the border strips. The border corners can also be mitred but were, in fact, seldom treated in this way. Medallion quilts have, in the past, been described as 'framed quilts'[9] but the American term for this design is used here to distinguish these quilts from the type of framed designs described on page 37.

Within the basic design plan of medallion quilts, an infinite number of variations can be worked. One of the simplest versions is the beautifully quilted North Country quilt in colour plate 2. Another medallion quilt with its series of patchwork and wholecloth borders (the most common arrangement) is illustrated in fig. 7. It was also usual to vary the patchwork patterns in each of the pieced borders: close links with traditional American patchwork patterns can be traced in these medallion borders.

The earliest documented example of a medallion design is an unquilted piece, dated around 1780, and illustrated in *Old West Surrey*.[10] A medallion quilt of a similar date is

9. *Border patterns for medallion and strip patchwork quilts*

known from America[11] and its style, both of patchwork and quilting, is so characteristic of the British tradition it seems certain that the design was taken across the Atlantic with the colonists from Britain.

The medallion design was used for both 'everyday' and 'best' quilts. For everyday use, roughly made scrap covers were pieced from cottons or woollens from the scrapbag. These covers show a minimum of organization; squares and rectangles of varying size are joined into a series of rough borders around a central shape (fig. 8). By contrast, carefully planned central medallion covers were pieced for 'best'. On these quilts, the size of the medallion centre and the border widths were carefully balanced and the patchwork patterns better planned to fit into the border lengths, but the sophisticated planning required to work a patchwork pattern around a corner was only rarely achieved. Fabrics, too, were chosen with care, albeit still largely from the scrapbag.

Medallion quilts, with covers pieced mainly though not exclusively from cottons, were made throughout much of Britain from the late eighteenth century through the nineteenth century, though there was a marked decline after about 1850. From around that time onwards, however, a new and simpler form appeared in the North-East of England, in which the covers were pieced in a restricted number of bought fabrics. Best known of these are the *star* quilts (colour plate 10), with covers designed, pieced and marked (though not usually quilted) by the quilt designers of Allendale and Weardale.

For the most part, patchwork patterns used in the borders of medallion quilts were simple combinations of squares, triangles and rectangles: some typical examples are shown in fig. 9.

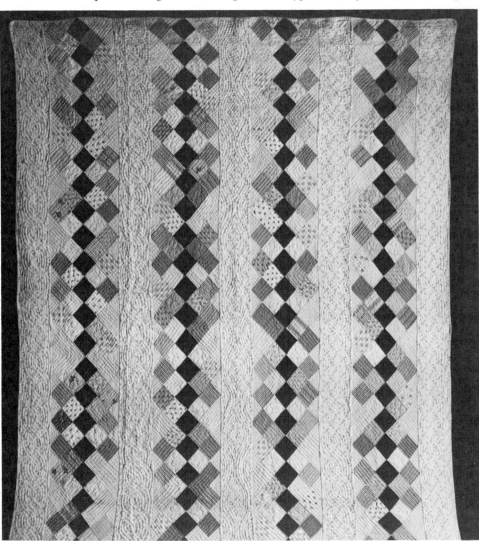

10. Strip patchwork quilt in multicoloured cottons made by Sarah Egglestone, Westgate-in-Weardale: c.1890 (234 × 188 cm—92 × 74 in.)

Some quilts did, however, include combinations of the shapes more commonly associated with unquilted 'English' patchwork – hexagons, diamonds, long hexagons and rhomboid shapes. When patchwork patterns were used for the central medallion itself they were often large pieces and of bold design. *Star* blocks were popular centrepieces but another common choice was to combine a large square, set on the diagonal, with triangles to make a large square centre block. Appliquéd motifs could also be worked on to these large shapes as on the quilt illustrated in fig. 8.

Although central-medallion covers were made throughout Britain according to the same general plan, the designs quilted on to these covers show apparent regional variation. Surviving quilts of this type made in Cumbria, the Isle of Man and the one surviving example from Scotland are usually quilted with simple *allover* designs using either *square-diamonds*, *clam-shell* or *wave* patterns. In Wales, the North-East and West of England, and Yorkshire, medallion covers were quilted with *strip* designs and *allover* designs which rarely had any direct relationship to the cover design. When a *bordered* quilting design was used on a medallion cover, it was more likely to be worked to fit with the cover design but not invariably so.

With the 'quilt revival' has come a renewed interest in medallion quilts, especially now that some carefully worked examples of this truly British design are surfacing from their 'holes' in museums and family homes. As a patchwork design it has many attractions for the potential quiltmaker. It provides the basic framework for making either simple or complex designs and for adapting and experimenting with different patchwork patterns within the border areas and the medallion centre itself.

Strip patchwork designs   A strip patchwork design has patchwork-shapes pieced into strip units running the full length of the quilt. The patchwork patterns can be of a single geometric shape (one-patch patterns) or a combination of shapes combined into repeated units (block patterns). The patchwork strips are often divided by strips of single fabric, but not invariably so. The basic design is very similar to that of a true strippy quilt, i.e. an odd number of broad strips, but with each or alternate strips composed of pieced shapes.

Strip patchwork quilts may pre-date strippy quilts but they were not a common type of patchwork design. Most surviving examples have come from the North Pennine Dales of Teesdale, Weardale and Allendale but rare examples have been found in the West of England. The same patchwork patterns used for the borders of medallion quilts were used for strip-patchwork quilts (see fig. 9), with cotton scraps making up the pieced strips.

Strip patchwork covers were usually quilted with either an *allover* design or with a *strip* design related to the design of the patchwork. They are relatively simple designs to piece and quilt, with no corners to work and no borders to plan. But with well-chosen fabrics, their simple, functional form is very appealing.

Block designs   A block patchwork design is based on a series of units or blocks with each block pieced in a particular arrangement of geometric shapes. Block designs can be made up from blocks of the same basic pattern or from blocks of different pattern arrangements. In practice, traditional British block designs used for quilts were mainly pieced from blocks of the same pattern, but blocks of different patchwork patterns were often pieced together for unquilted coverlets.

Patchwork blocks can be joined directly together 'on the square', with the seams running horizontally or vertically, or they can be turned 45 degrees and set 'on the diagonal' with the seams joining the blocks running diagonally across the cover. Two other methods of setting blocks together are found on traditional British quilts: (1) alternating patchwork blocks with blocks of a wholecloth; and (2) setting strips of fabric (lattice strips) between the blocks. Using alternate blocks of patchwork and wholecloth provides opportunity for working more elaborate quilting patterns than can be made with all-patchwork blocks (fig. 11). Block designs are usually framed with at least a single border.

Like strip patchwork, block patchwork quilts were less common in Britain than medallion quilts. They were certainly made in the early nineteenth century but cannot yet be traced beyond that with any certainty. A few were made in the early years of the twentieth century but, like other forms of patchwork, they were rapidly falling out of fashion by then. Late nineteenth- and early twentieth-century block patchwork quilts do show signs of American influence.

Block patchwork designs were rarely used for 'everyday' quilts – the precise planning and piecing required was too demanding for utilitarian needs. Some were pieced using scraps,

11. Block patchwork quilt in pink and white cottons designed and pieced by Elizabeth Sanderson and quilted by Mrs Adamson of Rookhope, Co. Durham: 1912 (239 × 211 cm—94 × 83 in.)

but two-colour combinations of bought cottons were more usual. As on strippy quilts, combining white with another colour was a popular choice: blue/white, green/white, pink/white and the favourite Turkey red/white, for example. However, one 'basket' quilt (*c.*1840) in the collection of the Bowes Museum, Barnard Castle, is of orange/yellow and blue printed cotton – an unusual and sophisticated use of contrasting colour in a traditional British quilt.

It is clear, however, from the evidence of unquilted patchwork coverlets that the patchwork tradition in Britain contained a large number of traditional block patterns. One coverlet, dated 1797, and now in the Victoria and Albert Museum, contains between 60 and

12. Block patchwork patterns

70 different block patterns in its design;[12] and that on just one coverlet! But only a mere handful of these blocks were apparently used on true quilts pieced in block designs (some are illustrated in fig. 12). Of these, *basket* and *star* blocks were particularly popular, with the variety of *basket* patterns providing opportunity to combine appliqué with patchwork techniques. Block patchwork covers are usually quilted with as much care as they are pieced. Quilting is either in an *allover* design or planned to fit with the patchwork pattern.

The block quilts made in nineteenth-century Britain were more restrained than their American counterparts but, nevertheless, do represent some of the best of British quilts. However, as the products of humble homes, they were less highly regarded in their time than the over-elaborate silk, satin and velvet patchworks produced by ladies of leisure.

Mosaic designs   Mosaic patchwork designs are pieced from single geometric shapes, such as squares, rectangles, triangles and the popular hexagons. One popular mosaic design in the nineteenth century, however, used two shapes – an octagon and a square (colour plate 3).

13. Framed quilt in cream cotton sateen (reverse, pink sateen) made by Mrs Stewart, a 'club' quilter, of Bowburn, Co. Durham: c.1910 (242 × 208 cm)—95 × 82 in.)

Mosaic patchwork was widely used in Britain for unquilted coverlets in hexagon and diamond patterns particularly, but quilted patchwork covers of this type used generally larger and simpler shapes.

Traditional mosaic quilts could be of wool or cotton scraps. One County Durham lady remembers quilts being made before the First World War of 'scraps of material, enclosed in pink and biscuit . . . easy to quilt, good wearing and washes well'.[13] Mosaic quilts in a restricted number of fabrics were also made (colour plate 4); like so many of the more carefully planned patchwork designs, this example had come from the North of England.

Quilting designs on mosaic quilts are usually *allover* or *strip* designs. It is not easy to quilt an elaborate *bordered* design on to a wholly pieced surface. The seams joining the pieces make it difficult to stitch through and, in any event, a closely worked design will not show to best advantage on such a pieced surface.

Framed covers

A framed cover is a simple but distinct variation of a wholecloth cover. Its distinguishing feature is the very large central area of a single fabric (usually of a solid colour) surrounded by a deep border, or borders, of another (usually patterned) fabric or of patchwork. Unlike the borders of medallion covers, the single-fabric borders of a framed cover are usually mitred.

Framed quilts of this simple type were not commonly made in Britain. The oldest known example is a mid-eighteenth-century silk quilt in the collection of Exeter City Museum. This unique quilt has a large central area of green silk with a deep patchwork frame of green and cream silk triangles. The border patches have sadly deteriorated but it was clearly once a most beautiful quilt.

Other surviving examples of this type are all from the twentieth century and, for the most part, appear to have come from County Durham where there was apparently a vogue for using floral-patterned chintzes to frame a cotton sateen wholecloth cover. Some handsome examples in perfect condition have survived, but the only two of known date and origin (in the collection of Beamish Museum) were made by women who ran quilt 'clubs' in the pit villages of Durham. Perhaps they arose through customer demand, for the patterned chintz used on the border frames was in keeping with the furnishing styles of that early twentieth-century period.

Framed quilts are invariably quilted with a *bordered* quilting design. It is the quilting design which gives the depth and quality to this type of quilt, so it must be well planned and carefully executed to create the surface pattern and texture otherwise absent from this simple cover design.

Appliquéd covers

An applied or appliquéd design on a cover is made by cutting fabric shapes of a chosen pattern, and stitching them to a larger fabric surface. Another type of appliquéd quilt – the *broderie perse* quilt – is made by cutting out printed motifs from one fabric and stitching them to another.

Both types of appliquéd quilt were traditionally made in Britain, where appliqué has a long history. It was in use by the Middle Ages, if not earlier, for banners and other heraldic devices[14] and later for wall hangings. Of these, the most famous surviving pieces are the sixteenth-century hangings in Hardwick Hall, Derbyshire, made by the Countess of Shrewsbury – 'Bess of Hardwick'. The earliest apparent documented use of appliqué on quilts, in the will of the Earl of Sussex (see page 158), also comes from the sixteenth century.

Surviving appliquéd quilts date, like most other types of wadded quilt, from the second half of the eighteenth century onwards. Like patchwork, appliqué was also used on unquilted coverlets – the styles of appliqué used on both quilts and coverlets differed little. *Broderie perse* was fashionable for quilts and coverlets in the late eighteenth and early nineteenth centuries, with motifs cut from Indian chintzes, or from block-printed fabrics manufactured in England. These were applied on to a white or cream unglazed cotton or linen ground, usually a wholecloth cover. At the same time, naturalistic shapes of flowers, leaves and even baskets of flowers were worked in appliqué in a style which imitates, to some extent, the naturalistic style of quilting of the period.

In the first half of the nineteenth century, appliqué was also used, as an adjunct to patchwork, on medallion quilts (figs. 8 and 79). Worked, like patchwork, in multicoloured scraps, appliquéd motifs were stitched on to the centres, borders and corner blocks. After 1850, a new style of appliqué appeared. Using solid-colour fabrics (mainly red and green, but also pink), appliquéd stems, leaves and flowers and, sometimes, the *Princess Feather*, were worked on to a white cotton calico or twill ground. These quilts are so directly comparable in colour and style to the 'red and green calico quilts' produced in America at much the same time that it seems likely that the British tradition was, in this case, strongly influenced from across the Atlantic. Though this vogue was short-lived, it did produce some bold and lively quilts (colour plates 5 and 6), especially from the North Pennine Dales and Cumbria.

Appliquéd covers were always intended as the top cover of a quilt and usually backed with a plain cotton or linen fabric. Where the appliqué is worked in a block design, a simple *allover* quilting pattern like *shell*, *wave*, or *square-diamonds* is usually worked over it. Where a medallion-style design is used, quilting may take the form of a *bordered* design planned to relate to the cover.

QUILTING DESIGNS

Any quilting design is made up of one or more pattern elements. Traditional quilting patterns can be broadly divided into *motifs*, *border* patterns and *infill* patterns; it is the choice and combination of these which go to make up the design. The quality of the quilting design is, therefore, a result of the careful and considered arrangement of the various pattern elements.

Few quilts were ever made with the quilting design identical in every pattern detail. One Northumberland lady, speaking of the early part of this century, pinpoints some of the reasons for this:

the people who wanted the quilts didn't want to have a quilt exactly the same as her down the road or somebody else. And if you were being married, well there was great competition about getting a better design on our quilt than you had on yours.[15]

But designs on most traditional quilts do conform overall to certain well-established design plans or frameworks. Although traditional quilters might wish to express their individuality, or rival their fellow-quilters by varying the choice of patterns from quilt to quilt, the frameworks into which the patterns were organized varied little. These organized symmetrical frameworks (designs) into which the quilting patterns could be fitted were as much part of the oral tradition as the patterns themselves.

In looking at quilting designs on surviving and recorded traditional British quilts, three basic design plans can be identified and these will be described in turn. It must be emphasized, however, that this grouping or classification refers *only to the quilting design* and not to any other surface decoration.

a   *b*

14. Allover *quilting patterns: (a) Welsh variation of overlapping circles; (b) North Country variation of* running feather

Allover designs

When a single quilting pattern or combination of patterns is repeated uniformly over the surface of the quilt, it is called an *allover* quilting design. The pattern used can be a simple filling one, like *wave, shell* or *square-diamonds*, or a more complex one. *Wineglass* and the larger *plate* version are popular *allover* patterns, worked either in the simple form of overlapping circles or with the spaces formed by the circle overlaps infilled in a variety of ways. Fig. 14a illustrates a characteristic Welsh variant of this pattern with the *four-leaved* motifs filled with line-infill and the spaces between with *spiral* motifs. In the North of England, popular *allover* patterns were *bellows and star* and *running feather* (fig. 14b).

Allover quilting patterns have a long-established history, though their earliest use may well have been on clothing. By the sixteenth century at least, they were being used on quilts,[16] but their purpose then may well have been to create a textured background for surface embroidery. Surviving wadded quilts, from the eighteenth century onwards, show that *allover* designs were mainly worked on to patchwork and appliquéd quilts, with the patterns used showing some variation from region to region. In the North of England and the Borders area of Scotland *allover* designs were sometimes worked on to wholecloth quilts. *Allover* quilting designs are simple to plan and are particularly suitable for quilts where the covers have other surface decoration.

Strip designs

A *strip* quilting design has the patterns arranged in broad strips, or rows, running down the length of the quilt. An odd number of strips is usually worked, so one strip runs centrally down the quilt. If different quilting patterns are used in different strips, the symmetry of the design is maintained by using the same pattern in equivalent positions either side of the centre. For *strip* quilting designs, border patterns are most often used, but infill or repeated

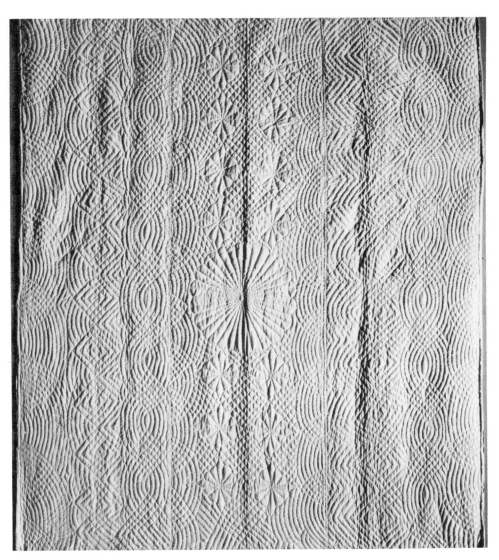

15. Wholecloth quilt worked in a strip *quilting design, North Country:* c.1910

motif patterns can also be worked down the strips. Double rows of quilting lines often separate each strip pattern from the adjacent ones.

Strip designs have come relatively late to the British quilting tradition and only appear on quilts made from the nineteenth century onwards. These designs are particularly associated with the counties of Northumberland, Durham and Yorkshire, but they were worked in Wales and the Scottish Borders, too. As might be expected, strippy quilts were usually quilted in a *strip* design, but so also were some wholecloth and patchwork quilts (fig. 15 and colour plate 4).

Strip quilting designs are easy to plan and mark, which is why they became so strongly established in the North Country tradition. Though many were of indifferent quality, some very fine examples have survived.

Bordered designs

Bordered quilting designs have a central quilted area – a central field – surrounded by one or

16. *Wholecloth quilt worked in a* bordered *quilting design, made in Pembrokeshire, Dyfed: early nineteenth century*

more quilted borders. Within this basic framework a number of variations have traditionally been worked, the most common of which is that illustrated in fig. 16. This plan has, as its focal point, a *centre motif* composed of one or more pattern elements. These can be a combination of motif and infill patterns, or simply a grouping of motifs. This centre motif is set within a *central field* of varying size, quilted usually with an infill pattern which, by its relative simplicity, focuses attention on the centre motif. In the four corners of the central field are *corner motifs*: occasionally, motif patterns might also be set (floating) in the central field. The central field is in turn surrounded by one or more *borders* of equal or varying widths. These are quilted with border patterns: if more than one border is worked then different patterns are usually chosen for each border.

This – the most characteristic *bordered* design – is the quilting design deeply rooted throughout much of Britain. Its form dates back centuries and was probably of oriental origin. As a quilting design, its basic form changed little until after 1850 when a gradual 'loosening' of the design, especially in the North of England, led to variations on the basic plan. Amongst these, the most notable was the dropping of dividing lines of quilting between the borders, central and corner motifs, allowing the pattern elements to 'flow' into each other. Some quilters also dropped the centre motif – the focal point of the design – and simply quilted the central field with an infill pattern (fig. 53).

Bordered quilting designs have been worked into all types of quilt cover but they undoubtedly show to best advantage on wholecloth or framed quilts. Medallion quilts, too, can look particularly well balanced when quilted with a *bordered* design planned to complement the cover design. The careful symmetry of *bordered* designs is ideally suited to quilts whose cover designs are based on square or rectangular outlines. On block or mosaic patchwork quilts, the lines of a *bordered* quilting design will conflict with the cover design, with neither design doing justice to the other.

QUILT CLASSIFICATION

The traditional quilting designs and cover designs described in this chapter have been defined in groups or categories for two reasons: firstly, to show that clearly recognizable design plans were part of the collective wisdom of traditional quilting; and, secondly, to provide an acceptable and understandable terminology for future description and discussion, and for relating the quilting design to any surface design of the covers.

In categorizing quilts in this way, however, I do not wish to impose a rigid structure on to traditional quilting and imply that any quilt, the design of which is rooted in tradition, has to fit into one of these groups. Boundaries between the groups are inevitably blurred and, if dividing lines were strictly adhered to, new forms would never arise. Though it may conform to a recognizable design plan, and show the basic symmetry characteristic of all traditional quilts, each quilt has some element in it which is unique – the essence of a hand-made piece.

3 Traditional Quilt Patterns

... the bumps are the pattern not the stitches
Mary Lough (c.1965)[1]

The lines of stitching on the surface of a quilt have two purposes: firstly, they hold the layers of fabric in place; and secondly, they give the surface decoration and subtle 'sculptured' texture characteristic of this particular form of stitching. In their decorative role, the patterns formed by the stitching lines are the basic and vital elements in the quilting design.

The patterns used in traditional quilting can be broadly divided into motif patterns, border patterns and infill patterns according to how and where they are used in the quilting design. In each group the patterns can be geometric – based on simple geometric shapes or outlines; or naturalistic – intended to reproduce, or represent in a stylized form, naturally-occurring or familiar objects.

How the many patterns now familiar on traditional quilts first evolved and came into common use is not known with any degree of certainty. Early documentary references to quilts, for example in household inventories, may indicate the fabrics used, but rarely the design or patterns. Only from surviving examples is it possible to make any attempt to follow changing trends in the use of patterns.

Many of the simple geometric patterns are forms of surface decoration common to a variety of artefacts produced over past centuries. Some can be traced back to prehistory; *wave* and *scroll* patterns decorate prehistoric pots and standing stones found in Britain. The ubiquitous *square-diamonds* (in general design terms called the *diaper* pattern) can be dated back at least to the ancient Egyptians who used it on printed textiles.[2] The border pattern *cable twist* or *lost chain*, as it is known to traditional quilters, is known to design historians as the *guilloche* and was in use in Assyria as far back as the seventh century BC. It also appears on the eighteenth-century quilt illustrated in fig. 48, confirming its long-established use in quilting in Britain. These geometric patterns are, however, simple in concept and need not owe their use in one place and time to any established use elsewhere.

The naturalistic patterns, on the other hand, seem to have evolved into a style clearly identified with their use as quilting patterns. The earliest surviving examples of wadded quilting, from the seventeenth and eighteenth centuries, contain patterns of variety and complexity which, whilst echoing the naturalistic forms of decoration popular in the textile crafts of the period, suggest a form simplified and adapted to wadded quilting techniques. Indeed, it is the patterns – both naturalistic and geometric – seen on seventeenth- and eighteenth-century quilts and quilted petticoats which seem to contain so many of the pattern elements later seen on 'traditional' quilts.

Once established as part of traditional culture, patterns were orally transmitted from generation to generation and from place to place. Though regional 'styles' gradually developed, well-known patterns could crop up almost anywhere. But of American influence in quilting there is little. Patterns were taken across the Atlantic by settlers from Britain but the American style of outline quilting, adapted for use on the wide variety of American patchwork designs, was rarely adopted by British quilters. By contrast, there is clear American influence in the patchwork and appliquéd patterns used on some quilts made in Britain in the second half of the nineteenth century. It would seem that the quilters in Britain thought their American cousins could teach them a thing or two about patchwork – but not about quilting!

What of the names given to traditional quilting patterns? Some names are short, down-to-earth descriptive terms like *plait, chain, diamonds, sea-waves, trail* or *worm* – no hint of the romantic or religious overtones which characterize some American patchwork pattern names. Others describe the objects from which the patterns are derived – *hammock* or *cap peak, dog's tooth, flat iron, wineglass* and the dialect *cuddy's lug* (a donkey's ear in the North of England). Some names have geographical or personal associations, like *Weardale wheel* or *Old Joe's chain*, whilst in the 1930s some patterns were given 'posh' names to please the buyers at the London end of the market. Mavis Fitzrandolph records, 'Once when I asked a County Durham woman if the name she used which struck me as rather highfalutin (I think it was *Roman armour* for the filling usually called *shell*), was an old name, she answered: "Oh no, but the ladies in London like it." '[3]

Some patterns had symbolic associations: various *basket* patterns were used on marriage quilts to symbolize a life of happiness and plenty. Two other patterns are often associated with marriage quilts: *lovers' knot* in the North of England and the *heart* motif in Wales. The same pattern might be known by different names in different regions – or even in different parts of the same region. Mavis Fitzrandolph records[4] five additional names for the common *rose* motif: *wheel, wheel of hope, whorl, Catherine wheel* and *boozy Betty* – though how it came to be called 'boozy Betty' begs a few questions! Some patterns have no known recorded names and, though I am reluctant to assign new names to these, it is sometimes necessary to use a descriptive term to identify them.

As with any tradition, most of the patterns associated with wadded quilting are long established and widely used, but the manner in which they are used can vary both with fashion and from individual to individual. It is possible to look at some quilts, particularly those made this century, and identify the maker. An experienced and skilful quilter will usually leave a personal 'stamp' on a quilt – perhaps the use of a unique pattern, maybe an innovative way of using a familiar pattern; or simply the way patterns are organized together (the design) gives that mark of individuality. 'Let's face it, each worker is an individual and you may use the same template but everyone gets a very different effect', commented one North Country quilter.[5] Any living tradition must be able to accommodate individuality and new ideas. With traditional quilting, it is the use of new patterns or new ways of using familiar ones, rather than the design frameworks into which they have been used, where gradual change, innovation and experimentation are most evident.

The stock of traditional British patterns is not large, for quilters were, on the whole, conservative creatures using the same basic patterns time and again. Many of the feather, flower, leaf and fan patterns and the *square-diamond, shell, wave* and *wineglass* filling patterns were in common use in all districts. But regional preferences did creep in: North Country quilters were fond of *roses, feathers, shells* and *cable twist* borders, whilst Welsh quilters preferred *hearts, paisley 'pears'* and *spiral* motifs with their borders still geometrically divided. Individual preferences for particular patterns are also evident.

When new patterns were invented they could be jealously guarded: 'some were very awkward and they wouldn't let you have theirs . . . if it was anything special'.[6] Others guarded their patterns in the often-mistaken belief that they were unique family ones. But such 'closeness' was fortunately not always the case; 'Quilters on the whole are generous with their templates and ideas, and generous in their praise of others'.[7]

When new patterns or styles did evolve it was usually from those quilters or quilt designers for whom quiltmaking was an important area of their lives, and not simply another domestic activity or pastime. Professional and itinerant quiltmakers and designers certainly contributed to changing styles and patterns as did those who established a reputation for the quality of their quilts. Social and economic pressures – making a prize-winning quilt for the annual (agricultural) show, or the need to devise patterns which could be worked quickly – could also result in new patterns and styles. Such pressure did not always improve the quality of quilt designs, especially if the pressure was an economic one.

Whatever patterns are used for traditional quilting and however few are chosen, they can still be combined in an infinite variety of ways. It is the way in which they are combined and repeated – the overall balance and contrast achieved between the pattern elements – which determines the quality of the design. Do not be afraid to create new pattern ideas or new ways of using established patterns. Surface decorations on other craft forms have been adapted for quilting for generations; contemporary craft forms can equally well be a source of new patterns and new styles of decoration. There has been a tendency in recent years for traditional quilters to become too parochial and unwilling to accept the use of any but existing patterns. Such parochialism has, fortunately, not always been the case: in the 1930s, for example, the young quilters in Wales who first learned to quilt under the RIB scheme (see pages 148–50) were strongly encouraged to invent new patterns, a positive stimulus which brought new vitality to Welsh quilting in those pre-war years.

MOTIF PATTERNS

A motif pattern is one which can be used singly or, if repeated, does not need to interlock with itself or with another pattern.

Most motif patterns hitherto used in traditional quilting are naturalistic ones. Simple stylized patterns representing leaves, flowers, feathers, fans, shells and stars have been found on quilts made throughout Britain for as long as wadded quilting has been a traditional craft (see figs. 17–21). More complex naturalistic motifs include vases or baskets of flowers: these were popular on eighteenth- and early nineteenth-century work, but passed out of fashion after about 1850 (see fig. 22). Geometric and symbolic motifs include the various forms of *spiral* patterns found on Welsh and West Country quilts, the *heart* motifs found mainly on Welsh quilts and the *lovers' knot* unique to North Country quilts. Examples of these are shown in fig. 23.

Any basic motif pattern can be varied according to how it is outlined and how it is filled in. Florence Fletcher, who learnt to quilt in Weardale in the 1930s recollected:

an old quilter . . . a Mrs Watson [of St John's Chapel] used to do beautiful quilting. I looked at her quilt, I said 'I've never realised before that you frame every template.' She said, 'Yes, that's the secret of making your work stand out', and no matter what [pattern] she put on, the outside edge was doubled. She double-lined it – and it works.[8]

Double-lining is a technique often used for motif outlines – it can help to delineate the motif more clearly. Triple-*lining* can also be used, particularly for large-scale motifs.

Once the basic motif outline is drawn around the pattern template, the area inside the outline is filled in chiefly by freehand drawing. Though leaf and feather patterns are usually

17. Leaf patterns: (a)
ivy leaf; *(b)* cowslip
leaf; *(c) and (d)*
Welsh 'bent' leaves;
(e) privet leaf; *(f)*
elder leaf

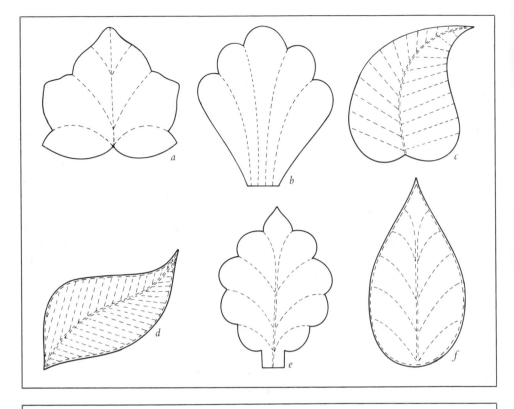

18. Flower patterns:
(a) daisy; *(b)* rose;
(c) North Country
tulip; *(d) Welsh*
tulip; *(e)* sunflower;
(f) thistle

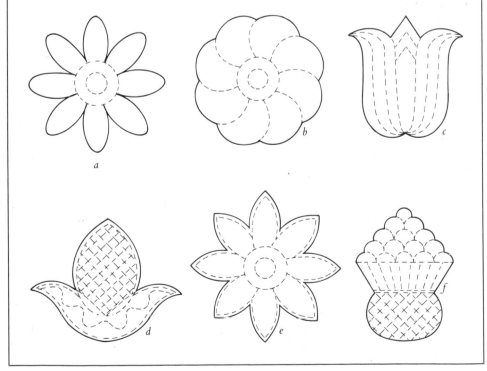

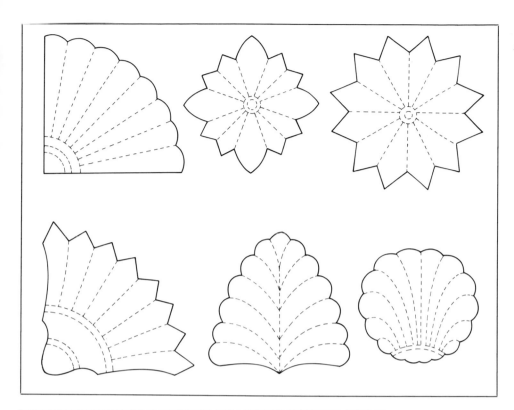

19. Fan, shell and star patterns

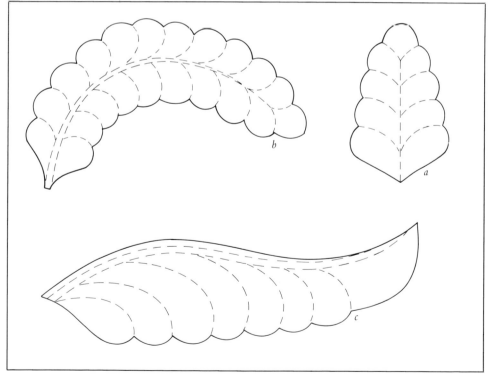

20. Feather patterns: (a) little feather, (b) feather wreath (use twice as mirror images); (c) goosewing

21. Miscellaneous motif patterns: (a) fleur-de-lis; (b) Baden-Powell; (c) rose and feather; (d) scissors (use twice as mirror images); (e) sheaf of corn (use twice as mirror images)

22. (a) Basket of
flowers pattern from
early nineteenth-
century West Country
quilt; (b) vase of
flowers pattern from
eighteenth-century quilt

23. Symbolic and
representational
patterns: (a) heart;
(b) lovers' knot;
(c) double 'S';
(d) simple heart;
(e) snail creep

24. Oval motif pattern with various infillings

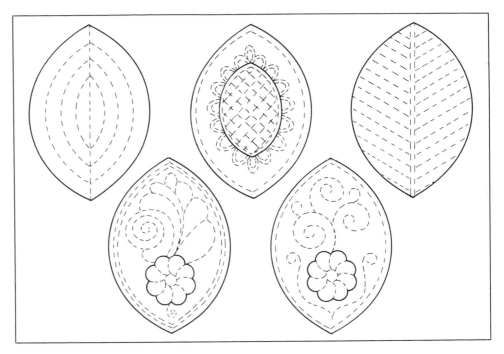

drawn in a standard way to show the respective vein and feather outlines, other patterns can be filled in more varied and imaginative ways; fig. 24 shows some of the ways in which a basic *oval* outline, for example, can be filled in.

Centre motifs   Most traditional quilts with *bordered* quilting designs have a central pattern of some kind set in the centre of the quilt. This centre motif can be either a single-motif pattern, like a *rose* or *lovers' knot*, or an organized, but always symmetrical, arrangement of several pattern elements.

On quilts made before 1850 two kinds of centre motif predominate: the naturalistic *basket of flowers* or *vase of flowers* of varying and often elaborate design; and the geometric *circle* pattern with a number of pattern motifs contained within a double-lined concentric circle or series of concentric circles. These naturalistic and circular centre arrangements were worked on early nineteenth-century quilts in all parts of Britain. Though the *vase* and *basket* patterns fell out of favour after 1850, the circular centre motifs survived, usually in a simplified form, on everyday quilts – particularly in Wales and the West of England. Indeed so widespread was this circular centre motif in Wales that Mavis Fitzrandolph records being told more than once that 'a Welsh quilt must have a ring in the centre.'[9]

In the second half of the nineteenth century, distinct regional changes occurred. Besides the circular motifs, Welsh quilters, in particular, devised other geometric central motif outlines but they retained a double (or even triple) row of quilting stitches containing the pattern elements and outlining the geometric arrangement. Some North Country quilters, by contrast, following the elaborate style of George Gardiner and his apprentices (see pp. 117–20), dropped the containing lines and allowed the centre motif arrangement to 'flow' into the filling pattern of the central field. It must be emphasized, however, that these trends were general ones. It cannot be assumed, for example, that a twentieth-century quilt, with its centre motif contained in a geometric outline, was made in Wales, for not all North Country quilters followed the 'Gardiner style'.

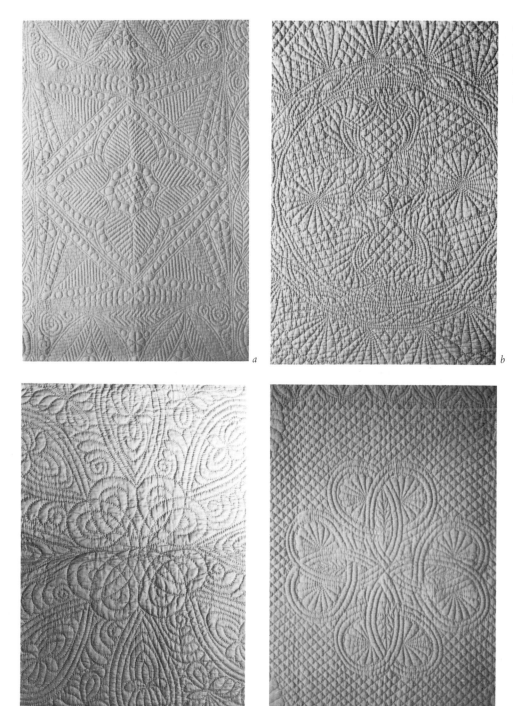

26. *Border patterns*

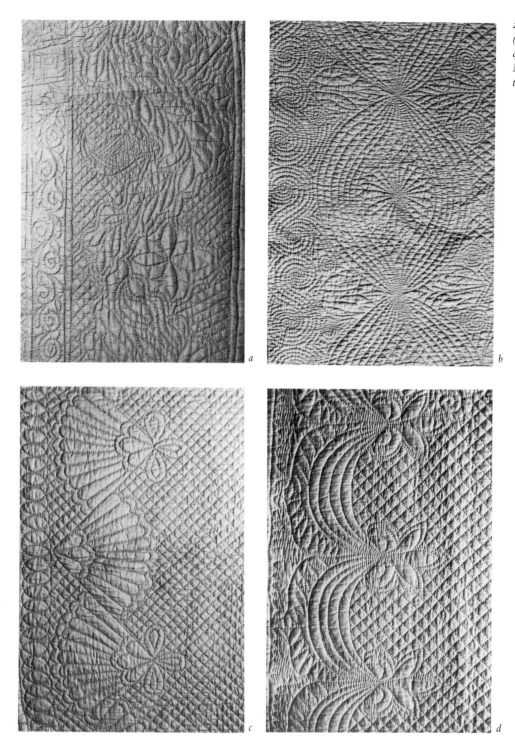

a

b

c

d

The centre motif of a *bordered* quilt is the focus of the design and the pattern elements of which it is composed need to be carefully worked out. It can help to plan a centre motif arrangement first before marking it on the quilt. This enables the quiltmaker both to judge if the pattern is a pleasing one when the chosen elements are put together and to work out the precise symmetry.

Corner motifs   On a *bordered* quilt, the corner areas of the central field can be quilted with a single motif or an arrangement of motif patterns. *Fan* patterns are particularly popular for these corners, because their quarter-circle outline fits well into the right-angled corner. But when bordered quilts have a circular central motif a quarter-circle of the central pattern is often reproduced in the corners, a feature particularly common on Welsh and West Country quilts.

BORDER PATTERNS

Border patterns are used to frame the central field of quilts worked in a *bordered* quilting design. Up to three borders may surround the central field, each of which can be quilted with a different pattern. Border patterns are also sometimes used to surround and contain the central and corner motifs of a *bordered* quilting design. On quilts worked in a *strip* quilting design, border patterns are worked down the strips as described on page 39.

Three groups of border patterns can be distinguished on traditional British quilts: (1) geometrically divided borders with the spaces between the geometric lines filled with either motif or infill patterns; (2) interconnecting or linking patterns like *cable twist*, *running feather*, linked *spirals* and the various chain patterns; and (3) repeated motifs, e.g. *roses* or *snail creep*.

There are almost as many border patterns as there are motif patterns: examples of the three types are illustrated in fig. 26. Other examples can be seen in the quilt details shown in fig. 27. Of the three groups of border patterns, the first two have a long established history and can be seen on the earliest surviving examples of traditional British quilting. Repeated motifs, on the other hand, are more likely to be found on later quilts.

On Welsh, West Country and the 'old-style' North Country quilts, the border areas are usually separated from each other, and from the central field, by double lines of quilting. On *strip* quilting designs, the border patterns are also separated by a double row of quilting lines – one line either side of the seams joining the fabric strips of a strippy quilt. But on North Country quilts which follow the style of George Gardiner, usually only one border pattern was worked and the lines separating this from the central field of a *bordered* quilting design were dropped (see fig. 27a).

Marking a border pattern accurately and, in particular, working it around a corner is a particular test of a quilt designer's skill. Patterns like the *cable twist* can be very difficult to work around a corner and it was not until the 1930s that a handful of North Country quilters acquired the skill to do this (fig. 67). Before that, motifs or filling patterns might be worked into the corner, separating the border patterns along adjacent sides. Advice on how to mark out border patterns accurately will be given in the relevant section of the next chapter, but some examples of how the problem has been solved can be seen in fig. 29.

INFILL PATTERNS

Infill patterns are used to cover the background of the quilt, that is, the spaces left when the motifs and borders have been marked. They have a practical purpose: when cotton or wool wadding is used, even the smallest spaces should be quilted to hold the wadding in place. No space more than 4 cm sq. ($1\frac{1}{2}$ in. sq.) to be left unquilted was the general rule. Synthetic

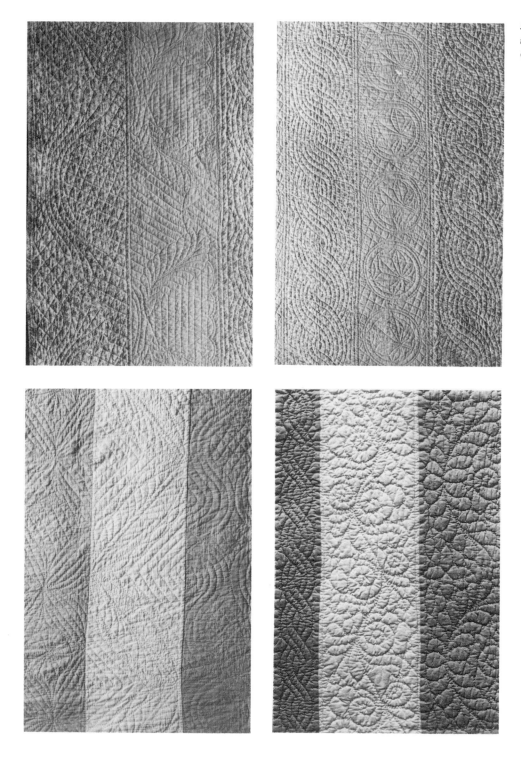

28. Border patterns
used on North
Country strippy quilts

29. Turning border patterns around a corner: four North Country examples (c.1910–35)

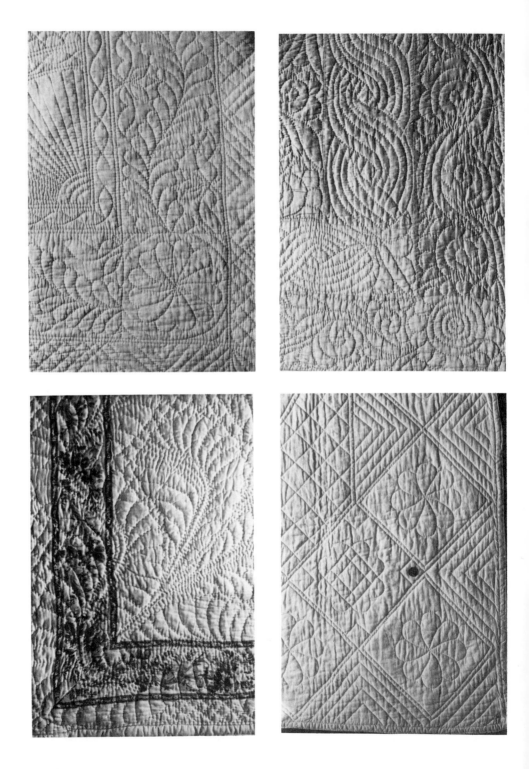

waddings, less likely to separate in washing, need not be so closely worked.

Infill patterns are also an important design element. Closely worked areas of infill quilting will recede visually (on a wholecloth surface), so focusing attention on the other pattern elements of the design. Many a quilt designer, otherwise competent, has failed to take account of this and used infill patterns too open in character to create sufficient contrast with the motif and border patterns.

The infill patterns used on traditional British quilts are, in the main, small repeated geometric units. Only five patterns have been in common use – *waves*, *shell*, *wineglass*, *square-diamonds* and *diamond* – but the history of their use as quilting patterns is a long established one. The inventory (1584) of Robert Dudley, Earl of Leicester, refers to 'A faire quilte of crymson sattin . . . all lozenged over with silver twiste'[10] – a reference, presumably, to the diamond pattern. Margaret Swain in her book *Historical Needlework* illustrates part of a set of bed hangings, dated 1699, quilted in a form of the *wineglass* pattern.[11] Though the quilting may have been of Indian origin, it establishes the existence of the pattern at that time in Britain. The other three patterns are all evident on eighteenth-century quilted petticoats and other quilted clothing, and on later, nineteenth-century, quilts. Of these patterns, *square-diamonds* has been the most popular infill pattern. *Wineglass* and *diamond* fillings were popular too, up to the Second World War, but *waves* and *shell* infills, much used on nineteenth-century quilts, are rare on twentieth-century ones in mainland Britain.

On North Country quilts, however, the apparent influence of George Gardiner led to the widespread use of *scrolls* or *curlicues* as infills on quilts. These patterns were mainly used to fill spaces in borders, centre and corner motifs, but not usually across the central field of a quilt. They were (and are) an easy option for space filling – drawn in freehand and at random, and needing none of the precision or matching up required for other infill patterns.

The five common infill patterns are illustrated in fig. 30. They can also be worked double-lined or even triple-lined – one well-known Welsh quilter was, apparently, renowned for her use of double- and triple-lined *diamonds*.[12] Other recorded but less widely used infill patterns are illustrated in fig. 31; of these *Scotch diamonds* was found on an 'old quilt made in Scotland',[13] and *Victoria diamonds* was named because it occurs on an eighteenth-century quilted petticoat in the collection of the Victoria and Albert Museum.

Geometric infill patterns were traditionally marked without templates, using rulers or the Welsh 'chalk-and-string' technique. Rulers, T-squares and measuring sticks are still useful tools for marking infill patterns, but it is now also contemporary practice to use notched templates for *shell* and *wineglass* patterns to achieve a greater degree of accuracy.

MAKING AND USING TEMPLATES

A stock of quilting templates for drawing basic pattern outlines was kept by all North Country quilters. To this stock-in-trade the quilter would add a variety of everyday objects as required – plates or wineglasses for the patterns of the same name, coins for marking the scalloped outlines of the *feather twist*, for example.

Templates were passed on through generations of a family, borrowed or copied from friends or neighbours, or made by the quilter. Though usually made from card or stiff paper, tougher materials like plywood or tin were also used: occasionally, they were 'just of brown paper or even newspaper'.[14] It was not uncommon for menfolk to be involved in the business of making templates (see page 109).

Welsh quilters (and most likely those from the West of England too) used fewer templates. 'Generally, the Welshwoman seems less concerned to preserve her templates, and you seldom see in Wales the permanent wooden or tin ones. More often they are cut from

30. Common infill patterns: (a) diamonds; *(b)* shell; *(c)* square–diamonds; *(d)* wineglass; *(e)* wave

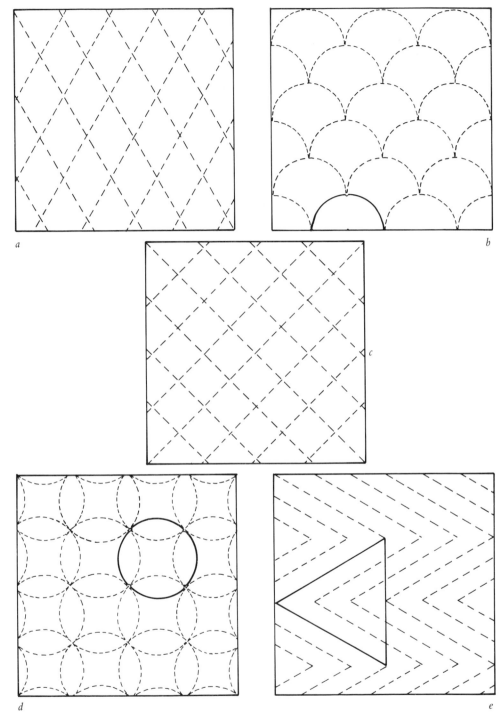

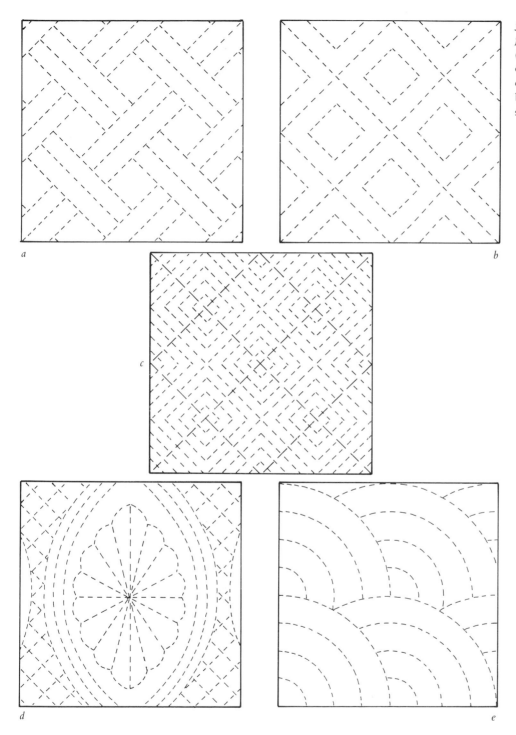

31. Other infill patterns: (a) basket; *(b)* Victoria diamonds; *(c)* Scotch diamonds; *(d)* bellows and star; *(e)* sea waves

a

b

c

d

e

paper to suit the quilt in hand.'[15]

For the quiltmaker today, patterns for templates and ready-made templates can be obtained from a variety of sources (see page 165). Most ready-made templates are available in clear plastic – a distinct advantage when marking overlapping patterns. Some organizations, notably CoSIRA, sell sheets of paper patterns which can be cut out and mounted on to card or stiffer material. But there is still something to be said for the do-it-yourself tradition of 'worrying away' at a bit of brown paper with a pair of scissors. Circular templates for *rose* and *star* patterns were produced in just this way by folding a circle of paper three or four times and cutting either a scallop or a point at the end – three folds for eight scallops or points, four folds for sixteen.

Many of the leaf, flower and feather patterns require individual templates to reproduce repeated motifs precisely. But some basic templates can be used to mark different patterns. Various patterns can be marked from a basic circle and a basic oval (fig. 32). It is useful for a quiltmaker to have these basic templates in a variety of sizes; whatever size is appropriate for the quilt in hand can then be selected.

32. Three border patterns marked with an oval template: (a) oval and diamond chain; (b) Weardale *chain; (c)* cable twist *or* lost chain

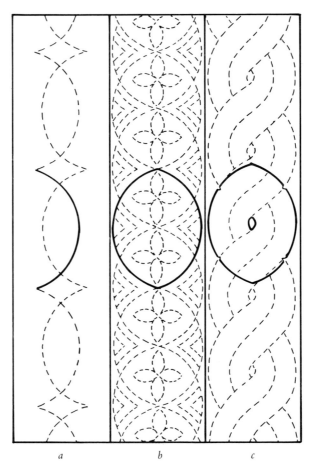

4 Making a Quilt

Quilting is 90 per cent perspiration and 10 per cent inspiration.
Old North Country quilter (1978)[1]

DESIGNING A TRADITIONAL QUILT

The first step in making a quilt is to think it out – design it. At this point the quiltmaker has
to make four basic decisions: (1) the size of the finished quilt; (2) the design of the covers; (3)
the quilting design; and (4) the fabrics to use.

Size   The finished size of a quilt will be determined by its purpose. If it is intended for use
on a bed, the size can be worked out by taking the measurements of the mattress (length by
width) and adding whatever drop is required for the sides where the quilt will overhang, or
where it might need to be tucked in. Cot or pram quilts, however, are usually designed to be
used (and seen!) with the infant sleeping peacefully beneath, so the 'pillow-end' of the
mattress is not covered. Measurements should be worked out accordingly. If a quilt is
designed primarily as a wall hanging (a growing contemporary practice), the space in which
it is to be hung will dictate the finished size.

Cover design   The design of the covers can be worked out in the mind's eye (the traditional
approach) or planned out on paper (the contemporary approach). Planning a design on
paper creates a visual impression of the finished quilt: at this early stage it can be
experimented with, adapted or altered, which is not always possible once a quilt is under
way. Patchwork and appliqué quilts, particularly, benefit from being planned on paper first.
There are so many variations that can be worked with even the simplest of traditional
patchwork patterns: the size of the shapes, the colours and fabrics to use, how to join the
patchwork units together are all variables, which should be decided before any stitching
begins. If this is done, by drafting out a scale drawing, then the quality of the design, in terms
of pattern, colour and proportion, can be assessed and, if necessary, adapted before the
quiltmaker proceeds further. (I would strongly advise the reader who wishes to make a
patchwork or appliqué quilt, and who does not already have any expertise in these two
crafts, to look first at one of the recommended books on the design and construction of these
types of covers.)

Quilting design   The plan for the quilting design depends on the type of design chosen, and
how it relates to the design of the covers. *Allover* designs and *strip* designs are not difficult to
work out; within the basic framework, it is fairly simple to think out which patterns to use,
what size to make them, and how to infill any spaces, if required.

A *bordered* design needs more careful planning, because greater attention needs to be paid
to the contrast and balance achieved between the pattern elements. This may be dictated, to
some extent, by the pattern of the covers if the design is to be worked on to a medallion or
framed cover. But if a *bordered* quilting design is worked on to a wholecloth cover, it is the

only surface design, and the stitching alone creates the line, textural contrasts and relief of the design. Few traditional quilters ever planned *bordered* designs out on paper first, but worked straight on to the fabric surface, following a 'design-as-you-go' approach. As Mavis Fitzrandolph recorded:

> Though the general plan is worked out in the [quilter's] mind before she begins, some details may not be planned until she comes to them; she may tell you: 'I'm not quite sure how I'll fill in that space; perhaps I'll put roses, or it might be pears.'[2]

Some quilters gave a great deal of thought to their designs. Mary Lough, one of the best-known Durham quilters (fig. 64) who died in 1968, often rose early to go for a walk. On her strolls through the Weardale countryside, she planned her quilting designs.[3]

For the inexperienced quiltmaker it is worth planning out at least some of the elements of the design. A simple scale drawing, showing the relative sizes of the borders, centre and corner motifs, will indicate, at a glance, whether the design is well balanced. It need not include the precise pattern detail – only the basic outlines. The centre motif should be carefully considered, before it is marked on to the fabric, because it is the main focus of the design. An easy way of doing this, without drawing out the entire design, is to draft a quarter of the motif on paper; then hinged mirrors can be set up in such a way that they reflect the complete centre motif.

Fabrics   When choosing fabrics for a quilt, both practical and aesthetic considerations must be borne in mind. The types of fabrics suitable have already been described (pages 13–14) so, bearing in mind these practical qualities, choose fabrics in a quality and finish suitable for the intended use of the quilt. Consider how well the fabrics will wash and wear, if a bed quilt for everyday use is planned. But quiltmaking is increasingly being used as a means of artistic expression, so the choice of fabrics – their colours, textures and patterns – becomes an essential element in the aesthetic quality of the quilt.

PREPARING THE COVERS

The preparation required for the two covers, top and bottom, depends on the designs chosen. Wholecloth and strippy covers are simpler to prepare than patchwork or appliquéd ones, which is one reason why they are more common amongst the quilts made in the late nineteenth century and the first half of the twentieth century. The preparation of the different types of covers will be dealt with in turn, but first a few practical points need to be considered.

The question of whether or not to wash fabrics before making them up is frequently raised. Traditional quilters were not in the habit of pre-washing fabrics: I have had enough negative answers to my question on this to be sure that it was not common practice. Indeed, the textural quality of cotton sateen quilts is heightened after washing when fabric shrinkage intensifies the 'bumps' and 'sinks' the stitches.

Patchwork and appliquéd covers, on the other hand, can suffer from unsightly puckering if fabrics shrink by different amounts. I would always advise pre-washing fabric to be used for patchwork and appliquéd covers, but consider it not essential for other types of quilts.

Piecing fabrics for the covers can be done by either hand or machine, using a suitable matching thread. Machine piecing became common practice for most designs as soon as domestic sewing machines found their way into homes (c.1860), for it is undoubtedly stronger; surviving strippy quilts, for example, are more often pieced by machine than by hand. Some traditional designs were pieced with a combination of hand and machine piecing; the central 'star' of the popular *star* design shown in colour plate 10 was pieced by hand, but the surrounding borders added by machine. Some rather pompous words have been written in the past, suggesting that machine stitching is quite unsuitable on any part of a traditional quilt, but this view is not now widely held.

Before any piecing is done, however, selvedges should be cut away – they are difficult to quilt through and the hard edges can show through the surface of the cover.

Wholecloth covers

Unless fabric wide enough for the intended width of the quilt can be bought, lengths of fabric will have to be pieced together to make up the full width of a wholecloth cover. Always avoid having a seam down the centre: it takes the eye away from the design and spoils the visual effect. Instead, one length of fabric should run down the centre of the cover, with lengths attached symmetrically either side of sufficient width to make up the required size.

In cutting out the fabric, do not forget to add seam allowances. Where edges are to be seamed together, an allowance of about 1 cm ($\frac{1}{2}$ in.) is sufficient but at the top, bottom and side edges of the cover, an allowance of 4 cm ($1\frac{1}{2}$ in.) should be added. This permits any necessary adjustments to be made when finishing the quilt, and allows for attaching the edges to the frame.

Use a flat seam to join fabric lengths and do *not* oversew or neaten the raw edges because this makes the seams difficult to quilt through. If stitching by machine, use a medium-length straight stitch – one which gives approximately ten stitches to every 2.5 cm (1 in.). If stitching by hand, a back stitch is preferable to a running stitch. Press open all seams after they are sewn.

Strippy covers

Once the number and widths of the strips for a strippy cover have been decided, they can be cut from fabric long enough for the length of the quilt. Only for the most utilitarian of quilts were strips ever pieced to make up the length.

As with wholecloth quilts, a seam allowance of 1.3 cm ($\frac{1}{2}$ in.) should be added at the edges where strips are to be joined together, but an allowance of 4 cm ($1\frac{1}{2}$ in.) should be added to the top and bottom of *each* strip, and to the outside edges of the two *outer* strips, to allow for finishing. Strips can be joined by hand or machine, but machine piecing will be quicker and less tedious. Join the strips with flat seams using a medium-length straight stitch and do not oversew or neaten the raw edges. When piecing strips by machine, begin sewing adjacent strips at opposite ends, as indicated in fig. 33, to even out any stretching which may occur and so maintain the shape of the cover. Once the strips are joined, carefully press open all seams.

Patchwork covers

Some of the varied patchwork designs used for traditional quilts in Britain have already been described and illustrated. Originally, most were pieced by hand, but a proportion were pieced by machine from about 1860 onwards, though fewer patchwork quilts were made in Britain at this time. The English paper patchwork technique, using paper templates for each patch and oversewing patches one to another by hand, was used for designs which included small geometric shapes, particularly diamonds and hexagons. This technique is still especially suited to piecing these shapes and the designs associated with them. Medallion quilts, on the other hand, were usually pieced by flat-seaming the patches together with a running stitch. This technique can be worked equally well by hand or machine.

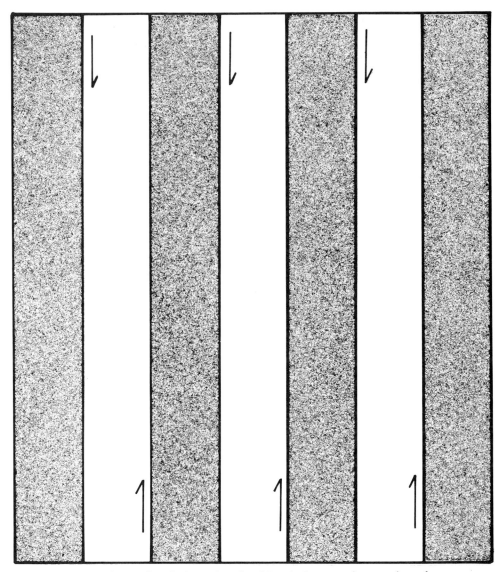

33. Piecing together strips for a strippy cover

direction for sewing strips together

The precise and varied techniques involved in piecing together patchwork covers are beyond the scope of this book and the reader unfamiliar with them is referred to the many books published on patchwork. However, the steps involved in putting together a patchwork cover, once the design has been worked out and the fabrics chosen, can be summarized as follows:

1. Pre-wash all fabrics.

2. Make any necessary templates for the geometric shapes in the design.

3. Cut out all the geometric shapes and border strips required, allowing 1 cm ($\frac{3}{8}$ in.) seam allowance on all pieces and strips.

4. Lay out the geometric shapes in the units in which they will initially be joined, e.g. blocks or strips.

5. Join the geometric shapes into the appropriate units, pressing open all seams as piecing progresses.

6. Join the pieced units together in the order appropriate for the design, pressing open all seams as piecing progresses.

7. Add final border strips as required. Press open all remaining unpressed seams and carefully press the completed cover.

Framed covers

When preparing a cover with border frames, the central area of the cover should first be completed. The precise method of attaching the border will depend upon the nature of the border itself, i.e. whether it is a pieced or single-fabric border, and how the corners are to be treated.

For a patchwork border where the patchwork pattern is intended to join at the corners, the sizes and shapes of the pieces should have been worked out accordingly so that the shapes at the corner link together accurately. Piecing can be by hand or machine, whichever technique is appropriate to the design, with a 1 cm ($\frac{3}{8}$ in.) seam allowance on all pieces *except* those which run along the outer edges of the border. On these pieces a larger seam allowance of 2.5 cm (1 in.) should be used on the sides which form the edge of the strip.

For single-fabric borders, the corners can be: (1) square cut; (2) mitred; or (3) have squares or rectangles attached to the border strips. In practice, the single-fabric borders of framed quilts were usually mitred (fig. 29c).

Appliquéd covers

Appliquéd designs on traditional British quilts are always worked on to another fabric surface; the technique of reverse appliqué was not, apparently, used. If the appliquéd design is to be worked on to small sections of the cover, for example the central medallion or corner squares of a medallion or framed quilt, these blocks should be first sewn in the chosen design before the whole cover is pieced together. If, however, the appliquéd design is to be stitched directly on to the full-size cover, this is first prepared according to design, and the appliquéd design worked on to it.

Appliquéd designs can be stitched by hand or by machine but if a machine stitch is used, the type of surface stitch produced needs to be carefully considered, so that it is in harmony with both the appliquéd and quilted designs. Most appliqué on traditional British quilts was worked, from necessity, by hand but some late nineteenth-century appliqué was machine stitched (fig. 60).

As with patchwork, a full description of the techniques used in appliqué is not appropriate here, but is fully covered in many recent publications.

Once the two covers have been prepared, they must be carefully pressed before the quilting design is marked and/or before they are set in a frame for quilting. All seams should be pressed open to make it easier to quilt across them. Raw edges should not be neatened for the same reason and because, if neatened, they can show through as ridges on the surface of the quilt.

PREPARING WADDING

Whichever type of wadding is chosen for a quilt, when laid between the covers it should extend about 2 cm ($\frac{3}{4}$ in.) over the edges of the covers. Some polyester waddings wide enough even for the width of a double-bed sized quilt can be bought, but if narrow-width wadding is used, it may need to be joined (it is advisable to join wadding lengths if hoop quilting). Edges should be butt-jointed to avoid an area of double thickness of wadding, and stitched together using a herringbone or ladder stitch. Polyester wadding needs no preparation except to make any necessary joins. Cotton and wool waddings, on the other hand, can need careful preparation. Elizabeth Hake describes the lengthy preparation required for raw wool:

About 2 lbs of wool would fill a large quilt, less than $1\frac{1}{2}$ lbs should be enough for a single bed size. It must be thoroughly scoured in soapy water, and after several rinsings, dried out of doors on a sunny breezy day, usually spread on the ground under a wire or fishnet covering to prevent it from blowing away. When dry it should still contain a proportion of its natural oil, which tradition claims, safeguards it from the ravages of moth.

Teasing or carding the wool is the next process, and a lengthy one. A pair of wire brushes . . . are more efficient and speedy than pulling by hand . . . All knots and lumps should be brushed out carefully, and the wool picked over by hand to ensure perfect cleanliness.[4]

Despite its excellent qualities, sheep's or lambs' wool is little used for quiltmaking today, for sources of cleaned and carded wool are hard to find.

Manufactured cotton-wool wadding was widely used, particularly in the North of England. It can still be bought, though now only from specialist suppliers, not, as used to be the case, from the local 'Co-op'.

Both cotton and wool waddings were usually warmed to allow them to 'rise'. Cotton wadding might also be picked over to remove the hard seeds or 'spleety' – a colloquial term from North-East England. The cheaper types of cotton wadding might also need to be 'skinned', as recorded by one Durham quilter describing the types of wadding available before the Second World War:

There were two kinds of [cotton] wadding; the white which was dearer. This would be warmed in front of the fire where it would swell and open more easily – or rise. The second type was unbleached and it was used for coloured quilts. It was also cheaper. It had a tougher skin and had to be skinned after it had fluffed up.[5]

MARKING OUT

Once the covers are prepared, the quilting design can be marked out. The design is always marked on the quilt top or, if the quilt is to be reversible, on the side on which the chosen marker will most clearly be seen.

Most traditional quilters did not, however, have the quilting design worked out in every detail before it was marked, though they would have in mind the framework into which the patterns were to be fitted. They would also have decided the relative sizes of such areas as the centre, the borders or the strips and perhaps made some choice of patterns to use. Some quilters might even have made a rough sketch of their intended design but a detailed working drawing would be most unusual. More often a mental image was the traditional quilter's starting point, and 'which pattern to use here and which there' was not infrequently decided as marking proceeded.

Opinions have always differed about when marking out a quilting design should be done – before or after the quilt is put in the frame. Mavis Fitzrandolph observed, 'on every point of technique there is some difference of opinion, but quilters are more inclined to be dogmatic about the patterns and how they should be marked than about any other point in their craft.'[6]

In Wales and the West of England it was common practice to mark out the design in the frame, though critical points, like the centre and border widths, were marked first. This method suited both the design, for the geometric style was easy to mark in this way, and the nature of the chalk used for marking. Chalk marks rub off easily and, if marking out was done first, there was always the possibility of lines becoming faint or even disappearing as quilting progressed. The Welsh method is clearly seen on the quilt shown in fig. 82.

In the North of England some quilts were also marked in the frame but these were usually the relatively simple *allover* designs or *strip* designs. Elaborate *bordered* designs were often marked out in full before the quilt was set in the frame so the quilter could be satisfied with the design before going on to quilt it, but this was not always done. Florence Fletcher said:

I like the whole thing designed before I put it on the frame, [but] my Grandmother she designed quite differently to the way I do. Now she would put all her materials in the frame and she marked it as she went on, but she'd done so many that she knew exactly where everything ought to be.[7]

The techniques traditionally used for marking out varied with time and place and, though most have now been superseded as better tools and equipment have become available, their practice should not go unrecorded. Welsh quilters preferred chalk (usually tailor's chalk), drawing around the templates to produce a not always very fine line. For circular motifs, particularly the concentric circles which often formed part of the central motif of a Welsh quilt, chalk was tied to a piece of string. In the West of England, chalk was also preferred, but in the North-East marking could be done with chalk, pencil or a needle. One quilt designer, still alive in Weardale, said 'I use blue crayon pencil, sometimes yellow crayon pencil and tailor's chalk to draw designs. On rare occasions I use a yarn needle to press out the design on the quilt.'[8] Needle-marking was, however, a popular method in North-East England in this century. The fine line produced by drawing firmly around templates with a sharp-pointed instrument, held at an angle, was easy to see on glazed fabrics and invisible when quilted.

Two unique and ingenious methods have also been described to me. One elderly lady from Gateshead, whose mother was a quilter, described a curious 'chemical' method: 'Mother bought some stuff from the chemist's and she used this to trace the pattern on the quilt. Then she set fire to it and it left a mark on the quilt for the pattern.'[9] Unfortunately, because the informant was quite deaf, it was impossible to elicit more precise information about this. But her memory of the technique was vivid, for she had once set fire to a whole quilt top when helping to mark it in this way. 'Mother' was not pleased!

From Sunderland, also in County Durham, came the details of a technique taught in a quilting class in the 1950s. A master template was made by pricking through a pattern outline on to stiff card, with a yarn needle, so that holes about 0.5 cm ($\frac{1}{4}$ in.) apart, following the lines of the pattern, were made on to the card. This master template was then placed in position on the quilt cover and pressed over with a hot iron. When removed, the rough edges of the card around the holes left a clear impression of the pattern on the fabric. My informant told me this technique was thought to come from Cornwall. She also told me 'Mrs Hoy [the class teacher] was criticized for doing it this way, because it wasn't the proper needle-marking.'[10]

For the quiltmaker today, the choice of when to mark out and what type of marker to use will vary with the quilting design, the design of the covers and the chosen fabric. Choose a marker suitable for the fabric of the cover and for the method of quilting (see page 21). If quilting in a hoop, mark out the design in full first. The method of quilting (from the centre outwards) makes a 'mark-as-you-go' approach less easy and the tacking lines needed to hold the layers together can interfere with marking. Be sure to choose a marker (such as a

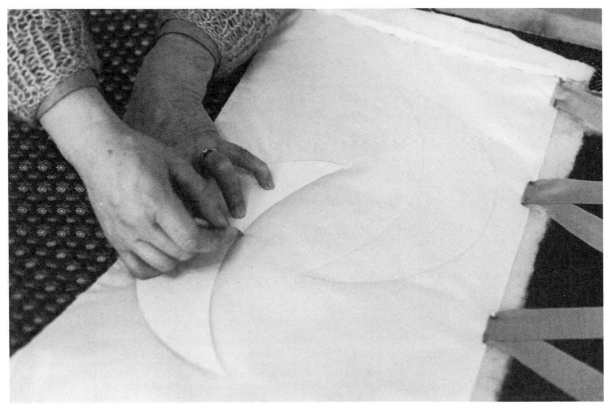

34. Marking out a strip design in the frame

coloured pencil) which will last through the constant handling a quilt in a hoop receives – chalk pencil is unsuitable for this method.

If quilting in a frame, some of the simpler designs can be marked in the frame, as can some of the designs whose patterns coincide with elements of the cover design – a strippy quilt or medallion quilt, for example. The patterns or lines of the cover design provide the points of reference on which to mark out the quilting design. But complex *bordered* designs are better marked out in full before the quilt is put into the frame.

Place the cover on a firm, hard surface, for example a table top, and draw out the chosen design on the cover. If needle-marking, place something between the cover and the table top to prevent scratching the table surface. A blanket was often used – I prefer a sheet of smooth card.

Marking motif patterns

Motif patterns of a design are usually marked in first, especially the centre and corner motifs of a *bordered* design. To do this on a wholecloth cover, the centre point and any border widths should be marked beforehand. On other types of covers it may be obvious where these critical points are. The following useful advice was given by a quilter in Allendale: 'first find the centre by quartering [diagonally]. Crease the lines then use these creases as guidelines for your design and for marking the diagonal diamond background.'[11]

Take the chosen pattern templates, place in position, and draw carefully around the outline. If arranging motifs symmetrically around a centre point, it helps to draw in a number of radii (equivalent to the number of times the motif is repeated) to act as guidelines (see fig. 35). If this is done, an easily removable marker or a line of pins must be used. Once

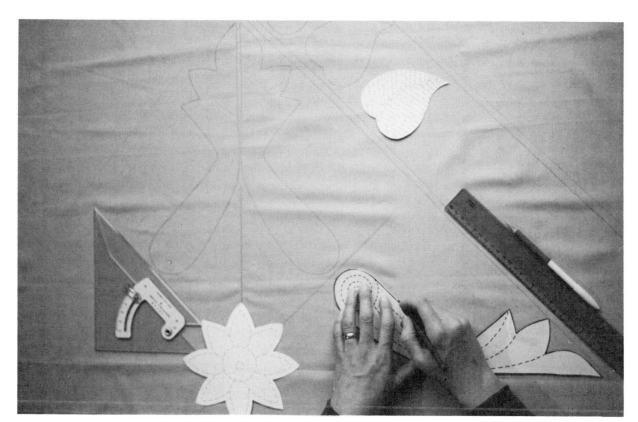

the motif outlines are marked, any freehand filling or further outlining can be drawn in. No great skill is required for this; with care and practice anyone can produce satisfactory freehand work.

35. Marking out a bordered design

Marking border patterns

Border patterns are marked in after any motifs have been drawn. A border pattern should fit precisely into the border length and not end with only a fraction of the border repeat at one end. It is clear, though, from many old quilts, that some quilters were either unable or unwilling to do this.

The method of fitting a border pattern into the required length of border depends on the pattern or patterns chosen:

Repeated motif borders   If the chosen motif does not fit precisely into the border length, the space between the motifs can be adjusted accordingly. For example, if a border length is 195 cm (76½ in.), and the motif pattern measures 23 cm (9 in.) across, it can be repeated eight times along the length. If the motifs were repeated with no space between them, 11 cm (4½ in.) would be left at one end, but this can be taken up by leaving a 1.2 cm (½ in.) space between the motifs and at each end of the border.

Interlocking or linking motif borders   On these borders the spaces between the motifs cannot be adjusted so easily to fit the border length; it is easier to make the border length fit the pattern repeat. First, measure the border pattern to work out the length of the pattern repeat (this may *not* be the same as the length of the template). Work out how many pattern repeats are required for the particular border area and mark the pattern accordingly, taking care to link the pattern correctly and to keep it running straight along the border. Care must also be taken when working different border patterns on a strip quilting design to ensure that each pattern fits evenly into the same strip length.

Geometrically divided borders   Geometric divisions can be worked to fit the known border length simply by dividing the border length by the number of divisions required (to find the length of each division) and marking this off along the border edge. When borders are divided into squares, rectangles or with overlapping zigzag lines (see fig. 26), then either an even or an odd number of divisions can be chosen. But when borders are divided by zig-zag lines into triangles, then an even number of divisions *must* be chosen in order to produce a symmetrical border.

Turning a border pattern at the corner is not always easy and was often avoided. It is now possible to obtain templates or template patterns for working the corners of some popular border patterns, though the *cable twist* corner can be drawn using the same oval template as for the rest of the pattern. For other solutions to working a border pattern around a corner, see the examples illustrated in fig. 29.

Marking infill patterns   Infill patterns look deceptively simple, but 'diamonds are the most difficult design to draw'.[12] Any geometric infill must be drawn in 'true', or it will spoil an otherwise good design. Guidelines drawn on to the cover help to fix the direction of the pattern correctly, but must be drawn with an easily removable marker, or marked with pins, if they are not integral lines of the pattern.

The problem of marking the *diamond* and *square-diamonds* patterns has produced some interesting solutions. From one quilter came the advice: 'cut the edge off a cardboard box, about 1″ wide. Use this!'[13] and from another, 'chalk the edge of a ruler and stamp it on to the quilt'.[14] Elizabeth Hake records yet another from the West of England: 'For marking squares or diamonds . . . a piece of fine string rubbed in chalk was extended from a pin at each end and when "snapped" up and down like a violin string would leave its mark in chalk clearly enough to be followed in sewing.'[15]

Shell and *wineglass* patterns are usually drawn in with templates; notched templates help to register the pattern correctly and keep it straight (fig. 30). If infilling small areas of a design, for example the areas of a geometrically divided border, begin marking these patterns at the broadest end.

The infill pattern called *waves* was restricted in use in mainland Britain, but was widely used in Ireland where it was marked with the help of a large equilateral triangle (fig. 30).[16] The triangle was used to give the initial, basted guidelines which could then be infilled with quilting lines about 2.5 cm (1 in.) apart.

SETTING UP

Before quilting can begin, the three layers of fabric need either to be 'set' together in a frame, or tacked together for hoop quilting, to ensure that the layers of fabric lie smoothly and do not slip out of position when being quilted.

Setting in a frame

Setting up a quilt in the traditional quilting frame described earlier (pages 17–18) is a straightforward process which seems to have been done in essentially the same way wherever quilts were made in Britain. It is best described in a series of stages with reference also to fig. 1:

1. Tack the bottom layer of fabric (the bottom cover, or backing fabric) to the webbing fixed to each rail (fig. 36).

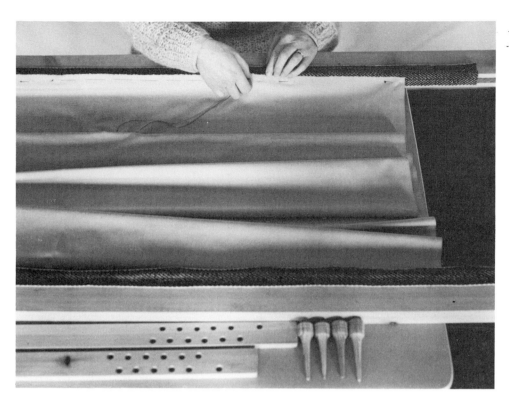

36. Tacking backing fabric to rail

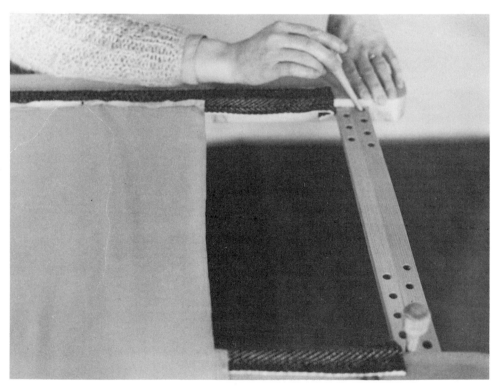

37. Setting stretchers and pegs in position

38. Laying wadding over backing fabric

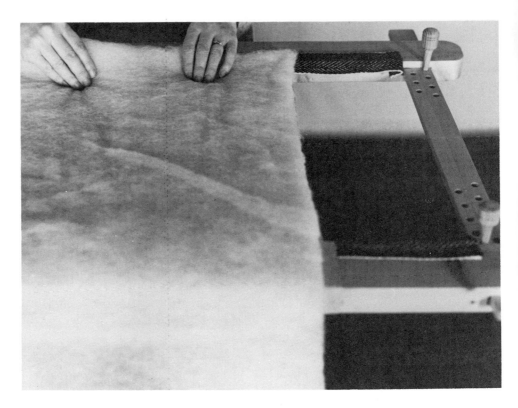

39. Attaching tapes to sides of quilt layers

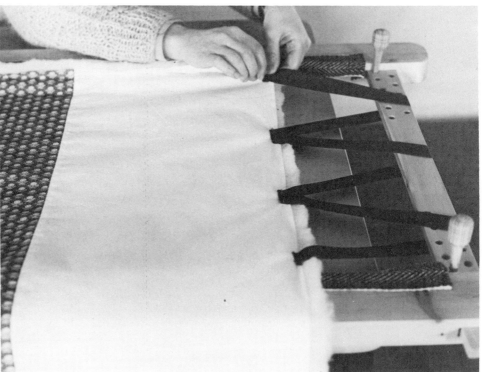

2. Roll the attached fabric carefully around the far rail (*b*) until a convenient working width (about an arm's length) is left unrolled.

3. Insert the stretchers (*c*) and pegs (*d*) in position so that the bottom layer is held flat (fig. 37) but not too taut.

4. Lay the wadding in place on top of the bottom layer with any surplus hanging over the far rail (fig. 38). If a narrow-width cotton wadding is used, lay the first width parallel to, and up against, the near rail (*a*) and quilt across this until the next width is required. This is laid on and the edges of the two adjoining widths teased out together to even out the join. If wool is used, lay on sufficient to cover the unrolled area of the bottom cover with an even layer. As quilting proceeds and the work is rolled on, add more wool as required.

5. Attach the top cover (and wadding) to the near rail (*a*) by tacking through the three layers on to the webbing. Lay the top cover carefully over the wadding, making sure it lies evenly and smoothly. Leave the unattached end to hang over the far rail (*b*) as with the surplus wadding. The top cover can then be secured along the edge of the far rail (*e*) with a row of tacking stitches or fine pins.

6. Attach tapes approximately 2.5 cm (1 in.) wide around the stretchers to the side edge of the quilt to keep the layers held firmly in position. Loop these tapes over the stretchers (*e*) and pin firmly to the quilt edges, with long fine pins, through all three layers (fig. 39).

7. Loosely roll up and pin any surplus wadding and fabric hanging over the far rail (*b*) so it does not touch the floor. Set the frame in position on its chosen support.

The quilt is now ready for quilting, with the three layers held firmly together. The layers must not be held under too much tension – there should be just enough flexibility to allow stitches to be made easily and evenly. Tension is adjusted by altering the position of the pegs holding the stretchers in place or by adjusting the pins holding the tapes in position: a little practical experience will soon show the correct tension to use.

This method of setting up is still used by quiltmakers today, but it is now usual practice on contemporary frames to attach all three layers to *both* rails and roll up the initial surplus on to the far rail. Contemporary frames usually have round-sectioned rails which make this practice easier (see fig. 2). The same system of tapes is still, however, used for tensioning the sides of the quilt.

Hoop quilting

If a hoop is used for quilting, it is essential to hold the three layers together so that the areas of the quilt not held in the hoop stay in position. Rows of tacking stitches are a simple, effective way of doing this; indeed, some quiltmakers tack layers together even if quilting in a frame.

To tack the layers together, first lay the carefully pressed bottom cover or backing on to a large flat surface, wrong side up. For large quilts the floor is usually the most suitable available flat surface. Place the wadding on top, making sure it is smooth and even, then lay the carefully pressed top cover, right side up, over the wadding, ensuring that all the layers stay smoothly together. Secure in position with tape at the corners.

Once the three layers are evenly in position, they need to be tacked together. Begin at the centre of the quilt and stitch tacking lines outwards to all four sides and diagonally to all four corners (see fig. 40). Then stitch parallel tacking lines about 15 cm (6 in.) apart both down and across the quilt, working from the centre of the sides out to the edges. Finally, run a line of tacking stitches all around the edges of the quilt to hold them in position and prevent the wadding from separating at the edges. Long tacking stitches – up to 7.5 cm (3 in.) – can be taken, but they should be firm, not loose.

40. *Tacking quilt layers together for hoop quilting*

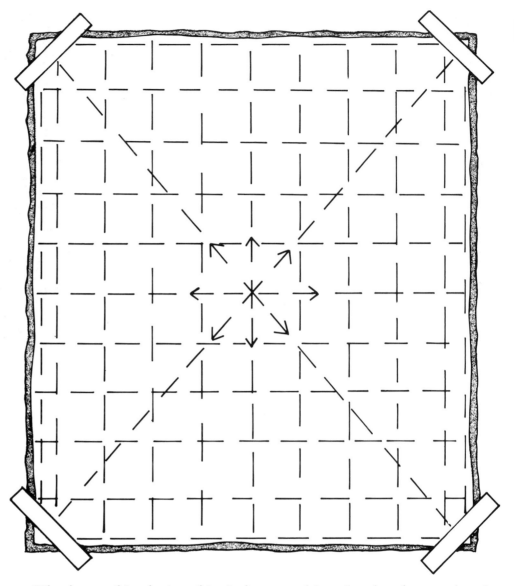

When hoop quilting, begin quilting in the centre of the quilt and work outwards to the edges. This allows any slight puckering of the fabric to be smoothed outwards. To place the hoop in position, unscrew the clamp to separate the two parts of the hoop. Place the inner hoop on the underside of the quilt where required, and fit the outer hoop over the inner one on the top side, making sure that the fabric is not puckered between the two hoops. Once in position, tighten the clamp to hold the layers firmly, but leave just a little flexibility to allow quilting stitches to be made easily and evenly.

QUILTING

Once the quilting design is marked and the quilt set in a frame or hoop, quilting can begin. The running stitch is the quilting stitch used on traditional wadded quilts; back stitching was used on flat and corded quilts, but rarely on wadded quilts. Running stitches look the same

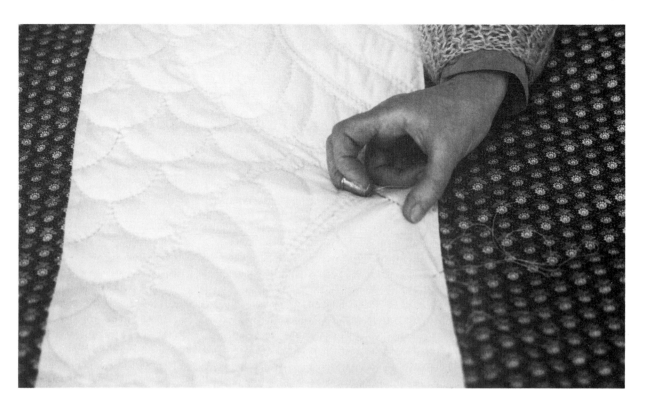

on both sides, allowing the work to be reversible.

Choose a suitable quilting thread. On most traditional quilts the colour of thread was chosen to blend in with the fabrics – white, off-white or cream on light-coloured fabrics; brown, buff, grey or black on dark fabrics. On wholecloth quilts a colour slightly darker than one of the cover fabrics was chosen. But some interesting effects can be achieved by using contrasting threads.

To begin quilting, thread a quilting needle with a length of thread about 45 cm (18 in.) long. Put a single knot in the thread end. Insert the needle about 2.5 cm (1 in.) away from the line on which stitching is to begin, on the top side, and bring the needle up on a pattern line. Pull the thread until the knot is held against the top fabric cover, then give a slight tug to pull the knot through the fabric. The knot should lodge in the wadding securely and not be visible on either top or bottom surface.

Keeping the stitching hand on top of the work and the other hand below, take even running stitches along the pattern lines. Use the middle finger of the stitching hand, on which a thimble *must* be worn, to guide the needle through, at the same time using one of the fingers of the hand below to feel the needle coming through below and to guide it back up. A guard of some kind can be worn on the finger below the work to prevent pricking. The thumb of the stitching hand is also used to depress the fabric ahead of the needle to help keep stitching neat and even. Like the fingers of the hand below the work, it will get pricked and a thimble can be worn for protection.

Several running stitches can be taken together before the thread is pulled through and, with practice, the quilter will develop a stitching rhythm, with the middle finger and thumb of the stitching hand working together with the fingers of the hand below.

The size of the quilting stitches often causes concern to beginners in quilting. Stitches should be neat and even in length with even spaces between, and carefully following the lines of the pattern, but the size will vary with the thickness of the wadding. It is easy to make small neat stitches if a thin wadding is used, but impossible if a quilt is thickly padded. As a general guide, if a 2 oz wadding or equivalent is used, try to aim for five to six stitches (counted on the top) per 2.5 cm (1 in.). The advice of Florence Fletcher is worth recalling: 'Nothing looks worse than spotty little stitches with big spaces between, but very large stitches will not make the firm line needed to outline the pattern.'[17]

When only a little thread is left on the needle, it must be securely finished off, so that the thread end will be invisible and not work loose. There are a number of ways this can be done. My preference is for the method described by Florence Fletcher:

When only a few inches of cotton are left in the needle, run it through the padding and bring it up, still on the line of the pattern; put it down again over only one thread of the material and repeat this until the cotton is finished. When a fresh needleful is started the new stitches will hold the end securely.[18]

In practice, if the thread is held two or three times after the last stitch, it should be secure, for it will be covered and held in place by the next line of stitches.

When working in a frame it is usually necessary to have several needles in use on the one quilt. Work along a pattern line as far as is comfortably possible, then leave needle and thread in position until the quilt is rolled and the next section can be easily worked. Stitching around tight curves can be tricky and it may be necessary to take only one stitch at a time.

Once the first 'arm's length' has been completed, the rails and stretchers of a traditional frame need to be taken apart, to roll the completed section on to the near rail, and then refitted together. Contemporary frames, on the other hand, usually have a simple rolling mechanism which does not require dismembering the frame. Once the first completed section is rolled on the next section is quilted, rolled on and the process repeated until the full design is quilted.

When quilting in a hoop, the technique of stitching is the same, but it is possible to turn the hoop so that the quilter can work in the most comfortable position and direction. It may also be necessary to use several needles: when pattern lines are stitched to the edges of the hoop, it is better to leave the needle and thread in position and continue when the hoop is moved to another position.

A quilt in a frame is left in position until the design is fully quilted but, if hoop quilting, the hoop should *never* be left on a quilt when it is put aside. If this is done, the fabric may become creased and marked where it is held in the hoop. Such marks can be very difficult to remove.

Quilting a large quilt is a lengthy process and attention should be paid to keeping a quilt clean whilst it is being worked. Traditional safeguards include: wearing pinafores and overalls; cutting the sleeves out of mens' old shirts, elasticating the top, and wearing them whilst quilting; and using talcum powder for sweaty hands. Of course a quilt in a frame should always be covered with a clean dust sheet when not being worked on. One Northumberland lady clearly remembers the careful attention to this problem given by the quilting group organized by the WI (around 1920) which her mother attended:

work worn hands . . . got rather sweated up with quilting, the talcum powder was the answer. It kept the thread clean, because if the thread in the quilting was soiled as it was being worked in . . . you couldn't remove it somehow. They wore old nightdresses back to front, these white nightdresses, so that they could be sure that they were clean . . . because you're inclined to lean on the frame as you're quilting . . . and if you have dark clothing on, as they had in those days . . . it would be soiling the quilt . . . And the rest that wasn't being quilted was covered up with old tea towels or an old tablecloth to keep the dust off and there was no smoking in those days anyway, so they weren't bothered with that. They wouldn't have allowed that anyway.[19]

MACHINE QUILTING

Using machine stitching for quilting contemporary quilts is a widespread and accepted practice. But machine quilting is not a substitute for hand quilting in the same way that machine piecing of patchwork can be a substitute for hand piecing. A machine-stitched line is a hard, solid one, much more sharply defined than the soft, broken lines of hand-worked running stitches. The character of machine quilting is much more in sympathy with the bold geometric lines of contemporary quiltmaking than with the curvilinear patterns of traditional quilts. Machine quilting traditional-style quilts has been attempted in various forms, with (in my opinion) a singular lack of success in capturing the quality of the hand-stitched form. Given the current 'state of the art', it is not a technique I would recommend for quilting a traditional quilt.

FINISHING

When the design is fully quilted and the quilt removed from the hoop or frame, the raw edges need to be finished to complete the quilt.

Most traditional quilts were simply finished in a way which is still appropriate for all quilt types. The method used is as follows: (1) turn the raw edges in, making sure the wadding comes almost to the turned edge, and pin together; (2) stitch two rows of running stitches along the edges. The first row should be as near to the edge as possible and the second row about 1.5 cm ($\frac{5}{8}$ in.) in from this.

On many North Country quilts these two rows of hand stitching were replaced by two rows of machine stitching, from about 1860 onwards. Quilt enthusiasts today are frequently puzzled by this practice for the machine stitching is often badly done   uneven and poorly tensioned. Why was it that a quilter could spend so much time and skill in hand quilting an elaborate quilting design, then finish with ugly rows of machine stitching? I can only try to answer this from conversations I have had with both quilters and their customers. The quilts finished in this way were often the work of professional quilters, especially the women who ran quilt 'clubs'. It made sense to them to speed up the finishing process by using a machine and 'anyway, it made a firmer edge', I was told. Customers seemed not to complain at the practice, but then quilts were such everyday bed covers in so many homes they were not, I am sure, the carefully scrutinized, treasured, hand-crafted possessions they might be today. Only discerning quilters and customers did not approve of machine finishing. The most noteworthy North Country quilters always hand stitched their edges, as did those quilters who produced quilts under the RIB scheme (see pages 100–102) for the London market.

The edges of a quilt were sometimes embellished in different ways according to the dictates of fashion. In the late nineteenth and early twentieth centuries, both frills and fabric triangles (now known as 'prairie points') were added. Frills, in particular, were popular with quilt 'club' customers, though they had to pay extra for them! In the 1950s deeper frills or valances were added, in keeping with the furnishing styles popularized in the women's magazines of the time. Piping was popular in the 1930s and 1950s and gave a firm neat edge. Bound edges, typical of American quilts, were not used on traditional British quilts as a rule, though they can be a neat and effective way of finishing patchwork and appliquéd quilts.

Not all of these embellishments are, to my mind, in harmony with traditional quilt styles. But such things are a matter of personal taste and the quiltmaker should feel free to add whichever finishing touch seems most in keeping with the design.

Part Two
Traditional Quilts: A Social and Cultural History

5 Historical Background

> . . . the final history must be written from all the collected pieces of evidence and put together as truthfully as the lapse of time will allow
>
> Averil Colby (1972)[1]

Like other textile crafts, it cannot be said with any certainty how or why quilting began; its origins are lost in antiquity. However, in most of the literature related to quilting, writers have made the assumption that the craft began in a humble way for purely practical reasons. 'Quilting', wrote Florence Peto, 'was born of the need felt alike by both rich and poor to protect home and person from bitter cold: it was based on the simple fact that three layers of cloth are warmer than one.'[2] She was by no means the first to make this assumption Just a few years earlier (1937), Elizabeth Hake had written: 'There seems to be no doubt that quilting is of ancient origin, arising from the needs of the peasant class, and developing in more elaborate forms for prosperous members of the community as fashion dictated.'[3]

As I have looked at the available evidence, I have come increasingly to question this assumption. Both recorded history and surviving quilts and quilted items suggest, for the most part, an association not with a peasant class but with higher levels of society – until the eighteenth century. The surviving evidence begs a few questions. If quilts were made by humble peasants for warmth, why are many, especially the earliest examples, so thinly wadded or even have no wadding at all? Why were they often made of fragile fabrics like silk? Why are they so intricately stitched when such stitching, for all practical purposes, reduces their insulation? And why is there so little evidence of a quilting tradition amongst the peasant communities in parts of the world where the need for protection against the cold would be greatest, for example Scandinavia?

I now believe that, although quilting is indeed an ancient craft, the assumption that its origin was in a peasant or working class cannot be supported from available evidence. Indeed, for wadded quilts themselves, evidence points in the opposite direction and though they have undoubtedly been made by men and women at all levels of society, at various times in the past, what we now know points to a gradual move 'down' the social scale rather than 'up'.

It could be argued, of course, that the evidence we have shows a distinct bias. Little attention has been paid in the past to the lives of ordinary people – particularly in Britain. 'Most history is concerned with [the] minority, who owned most of the wealth, exercised supreme power, and made all important decisions in the country.'[4] So documents, artefacts and records of all kind relate mainly to this affluent minority which at best made up only 30 per cent of the population of Britain and at times, less than 10 per cent. By contrast, the 'peasant who owned no real property and very little personal property, made no records and scarcely provoked others to put pen to parchment or paper except to record his crimes and misdemeanours, his succession to his father's property and his disappearance from his narrow earthly scene.'[5]

Whilst accepting this historical bias, I still believe that enough evidence exists, particularly from 'succession to property', to suggest that quilts had no significant place in the *domestic* lives of the common British people until the eighteenth century. So we must look again, separating fact from romanticism, to see how the wadded quilt established itself in Britain as a form of bed covering first, I believe, in the palace or castle, then in the country house, manor and, eventually, cottage.

EARLY ORIGINS

It is generally assumed that the craft of quilting reached Britain during the period of the Crusades. It is not an unreasonable assumption: the first evidence for quilting in Britain appears in the Middle Ages but, at this time, decorative needlecrafts, including quilting, were widely used in Middle and Far Eastern countries. Quilting already had a long history dating back probably 5000 years: carved figures from ancient Mediterranean civilizations show sophisticated embroidery patterns on elements of dress, some of which suggest quilting.[6]

The earliest known surviving example of quilting, a carpet now in the Leningrad Department of the Institute of the Academy of Science of the USSR, dates from the period between 100 BC and 200 AD. Found in a tomb in northern Mongolia during an expedition in 1924/5, it is undoubtedly 'the work of an embroiderer expert in stitching and using it with consummate skill'.[7] So, before quilting was first introduced into Britain, it was already a highly developed form of needlework in the Middle and Far East. In England, embroiderers famed for the quality of their ecclesiastical work, *Opus Anglicanum*, would have had little difficulty in adapting to the techniques of quilting. However, the first direct evidence for quilting in Britain relates to its use not for bed quilts but for padded armour: 'a fairly consistent picture can be built up from records, inventories and the works of contemporary writers and poets, of the uses and construction of quilted armour, from the time of William the Conqueror and the Crusades at the end of the eleventh century.'[8]

1200–1600

For the period 1200–1600, quilts known to have been made in Britain have not survived. It is from historical records (particularly inventories), and contemporary writings that a consistent picture emerges of the use of quilting for bed quilts, amongst other uses. Medieval taxation was based on property so, from the late thirteenth century onwards, inventories of household goods were made to provide the basis for this. These household inventories give most of the information about the nature and use of quilts in Britain for the period up to 1600.

The *Oxford English Dictionary* records the earliest mention of a quilt in a document of 1290: 'Maketh a bed . . . of quoiltene and of meterasz'; this does suggest the use of a quilt as a top covering. Another entry (*c.*1320) records 'Foure hondred beddes of sect echon, Quiltes of gold (there) upon'. The fourteenth-century romance *Ywayne and Gawaine* contains the following lines:

> And she did sit upon his bed
> A quylt ful nobil lay thoreon
> Richer saw he never none[9]

In the *Romance of Arthur of lytel Brytayne*, also a fourteenth-century work, a 'rich quilt wrought with coten, with crimson sendel [silk] stitched with thredes of gold' is mentioned.[10] These early references tell us nothing of the quilting techniques used but they do indicate the nature of the materials both for the quilts themselves and for their decoration. The use of expensive materials suggests an association with wealth and nobility.

Fifteenth-century references to quilts are rare, though further research could bring more to light. In wills and inventories of the northern counties of England, published by the Surtees Society, mention is made in the Durham Account Rolls (1454) of 'ij qwhiltez . . . j whilte' and in the Ripon Chapter Acts (1477) of 'unum twylt'. The use of the word 'twylt' at such an early time is of particular interest for it remained in use, as a dialect word, in North-East England for almost another 500 years. Surviving quilters can recall its use for quilts in their young days.

In the sixteenth century, references to quilts in wills and inventories become more frequent, though they only appear in documents belonging to the aristocracy, gentry or wealthy merchants (see Appendix, page 158). Descriptions, sometimes lengthy, provide some insight into both the nature of the quilts themselves and their worth to the household. It becomes apparent that quilts of rich and expensive fabrics, vivid colours and ornate decoration were to be found on the beds of the most important members of upper-class and newly emerging wealthy middle-class families. In rare entries, a monetary value is given to a quilt: the inventory (1592) of Sir John Parrot of Carew Castle, Pembrokeshire, includes a value of 20 shillings (£1) for a 'changeable silk quilt', and the same value is given to two 'old quiltes of yellowe sercuet'.[11] A few years earlier (1597) a value of 6s 8d (33p) was put on a quilt owned by William Teneson of Newcastle.[12] No doubt value would depend on condition and it seems unlikely that these quilts, having been in use for at least some time, would be in perfect condition. They nevertheless represent a value considerably in excess of a working man's weekly wage at the time.

Where the quilts that adorned the beds of royalty, aristocracy and the very wealthy were made is not recorded. Some were almost certainly imported – close trading and cultural links with Europe had existed for centuries and imports had included quilts. One quilt valued at 3s 4d (17p) was included in the cargo of one of the 'innumerable little boats' plying between Cornwall and the Breton ports.[13] Trading links with the Near and Far East also existed and quilts were almost certainly imported from this source. But it seems equally possible that some were made in Britain for quilting was, by the sixteenth century, an established trade: the *Fugitive Tracks* list of 1563[14] includes 'Broyderers, Taylors, Quylters and Limners'. To support such a professional trade, quilting must have been in widespread use. It was in practical use for padded armour, padded jackets and for quilted caps worn both by day and by night (it was considered that to cover the head was conducive to good health[15]). Its use on bed quilts was probably more decorative than practical, though wadded quilts were certainly in existence by the end of the sixteenth century and maybe their use combined a degree of warmth with show. Quilted day clothes, however, had not yet reached the level of fashion they were to attain in the subsequent two centuries.

By 1600, it seems unlikely that quilting was solely in the hands of professional quilters. Amateur needlework was an important pastime for noble and wealthy women, relieved from domestic chores. Moreover, bed furnishings were much-prized domestic possessions, often of greater value than all other household belongings put together. Much time and skill was spent on producing ornate bed furnishings; many were no doubt produced domestically by the women of the household or the servants, and the standard of this amateur work was often as high as that of professionals.

If quilts were also made domestically, in humble homes as a means of providing warm bed covers and warm clothing, the period up to the close of the sixteenth century should provide at least some evidence. Inventories of peasants' goods for this period are rare but those that do exist serve only to highlight the scanty possessions of the peasant class. At night, they slept either on the floor or on constructed frames around the walls of a single-roomed or, at the most, a two-roomed dwelling-house. Mattresses were of straw or flock, though occasionally a feather bed (a great luxury) is mentioned.[16] People slept under coarse linen sheets of home-grown flax or hemp, and blankets and rugs woven from sheep's wool. In a largely self-sufficient or barter economy, they provided for their material needs by their own labours. In his book *The Midland Peasant*, W. G. Hoskins details some of the possessions of sixteenth-century peasants:[17] Robert Frere died in 1529 and left, in his *two*-roomed house, 'furnishings and household goods meagre in the extreme . . . In the parlour stood a bedstead . . . and on the bed lay an old mattress and blanket.' In 1564, Thomas Reddeley died in possession of 'two old cows, two coverlets, a pot and a pan'. This sparse picture is confirmed by William Harrison; in 1577 he wrote in *Elizabethan England*:

Our fathers and we ourselves have lyen full ofte upon straw pallettes, covered only with a sheet, under coverlets of dagswain or hop harlots . . . and a good round logge under their heedes, instead of a boulster. If it were so that our fathers or the good men of the house had . . . a mattress or flock bed and thereto a sacke of chafe to rest hys heeds upon, he thought himself to be well loged as the lorde of the towne, so well were they contented . . . As for servants, if they had any sheete above them, it was well, for seldome had they any under their bodies, to keep them from the pricking straws that ranne oft thorow the canvas . . .[18]

Though Harrison's comment was somewhat scornful of 'soft luxuries', he nevertheless illustrates the meagre nature of the beds and bedding of most common people – even the yeoman class – until around 1550. Harrison was also commenting on a change which was rapidly taking place. England, under Elizabeth I, increased notably in prosperity – between 1550 and 1600 material standards almost doubled. By the closing years of the sixteenth century 'the standard of household furnishing and comforts to life had very markedly improved among all classes of peasant community',[19] but there is still no evidence that quilts formed any part of their usual possessions.

The close of the sixteenth century is an appropriate place to pause and consider the position and role of quilting up to the final years of Elizabethan England. As a technique it had been established in Britain for over 500 years. It had been and was still used for some forms of clothing: padded jackets for winter warmth, petticoats 'of lynen clothe stoffyd with flockys' (from an inventory of 1459)[20] and quilted caps. No doubt these formed part of the stock-in-trade of the professional quilters, well-established in a small but recognized trade.

For quilts themselves, quilting was used on expensive and ornate bed covers. Quilts were often part of the lavish and much-prized bed furnishings of royalty, nobility and also wealthy merchants. It seems, though, that they were not to be found in the houses of common people for, despite the increasing prosperity which came with the Elizabethan age, the gulf between the rich and poor, in terms of household possessions, was an enormous one.

SEVENTEENTH CENTURY

The seventeenth century, one of turmoil in Britain, was one of some significance for quilting. By now well established as a textile trade, fashion trends led to its increased use for all kinds of garments and for a variety of upholstery and furnishing uses – especially bed quilts. Much information about seventeenth-century quilts still comes from written sources; wills, inventories and now wardrobe accounts show that materials of quality continued to be used. Quilts in varieties of silk and satin, some brightly coloured, adorned the beds in fashionable homes, but more neutral tones, such as cream or ivory, were also used. Linen quilts became increasingly common; they were often flat-quilted, indicating a decorative rather than a practical function despite the more hard-wearing nature of the material.

42. *Detail of quilted satin doublet thought to have been made from a quilt; English: 1635–40*

Wadded quilts, wool-filled, continued to be made: three quilts 'of fustian, lined with taffeta, filled with wool and sewed with silk' were given by James I to his daughter Princess Elizabeth on the occasion of her marriage in 1609.[21]

A number of examples of English quilting from the seventeenth century have survived. One of the earliest pieces is the doublet and jacket, now in the Victoria and Albert Museum, London, supposedly made from a cut-down wadded quilt (fig. 42). The style of quilting is characteristic of that seen on wadded quilts and clothing in the seventeenth and eighteenth centuries, so difficult to date precisely. But the style of dress – a better chronological indicator – dates the two pieces to the reign of Charles I, 1635–40. Another late seventeenth-

43. Detail of white quilted silk jacket; English: late seventeenth century

century piece, a quilted jacket, is in similar style (fig. 43). Worked in running stitch on silk, the organization of the design, the simple stylized leaf and flower patterns, and the filling pattern all show the characteristics of what later became traditional quilting.

Other surviving examples of seventeenth-century quilting include flat-quilted linen pillow shams, used as day-time covers for pillows. Though of Indo-Portuguese influence, one English example also in the Victoria and Albert Museum is of particular interest.[22] The style of its closely worked backstitching is different from the running stitchery of wadded quilting but the pattern worked on to this piece, and the disposition of the design, are both typical of traditional quilting. Here are all the common filling patterns – *wave*, *shell*, *wineglass* and *square-diamonds* – together with *cable twist* and *church window* borders. Only the carefully drawn, almost art nouveau centre is untypical of traditional quilt style.

The nature of these surviving pieces confirms that, by the seventeenth century, the style and basic pattern-stock of traditional quilting was already in existence in Britain. And it was not a uniquely British style – the Portuguese quilt in the Victoria and Albert Museum's *Notes on Quilting*[23] shows close similarities in style and the arrangement of its border patterns, in particular. How far back the style and techniques go it is difficult to say with any certainty, and where they came from. There were close cultural links between the southern counties of England and the continent of Europe, but there was also contact with the Near and Far East. There is undoubtedly oriental influence in the organization of the design of quilts but how far this was tempered to British or European taste is another question.

It is not certain who made these quilts and quilted garments. Professional quilters, probably based around London, were still at work;[24] it is also possible that professionals were engaged to draw the design onto quilts and garments, a practice recorded in the next century. Pattern sheets for embroidery are known to have been on sale in the seventeenth century[25] – perhaps quilting patterns were similarly available. Domestic quilting in country houses and manor houses was almost certainly a common practice, for amateur embroiderers were no doubt as well able to use their skills for quilting as they were for working samplers and embroidered pictures.

One important factor in the increasing popularity of quilts in the seventeenth century – and one which was to have far-reaching consequences for the British textile industry as a whole – was the growth in trade with India. In 1600 the English East India Company was formed, three years after the formation of its Dutch counterpart. The interest of both companies was not initially in textiles but in pepper and spices from the Malay archipelago. The people of the Spice Islands were, however, very primitive and some kind of barter goods, rather than bullion, were required to exchange for the precious spices. Indian piece-goods proved acceptable, so a three-cornered trade developed: ships sailing from Europe with bullion exchanged this for Indian textiles which were, in turn, exchanged for spices in the Malay archipelago.

Small quantities of Indian textiles reached England from 1613 onwards and they were much coveted as novelties. The suitability of Indian textiles for quilts was recognized as early as 1609. Writing from Surat in that year, a merchant reported that 'Pintadoes of all sorts, especially the finest . . . I mean such as are for quilts and for fine hangings' are 'brought from a place called Brampore';[26] but their import was not allowed until the Royal Proclamation of Charles I in 1635. Later, in 1643, 'Pintadoe Quilts' were imported and put on sale; they fetched a price of 50s (£2.50) each but this was considered disappointing, so instructions were sent to the agent in Surat suggesting adaptation of the design to Western taste.[27] The results were successful and 'within the next five years auction prices in London increased by 20 per cent and orders had grown twentyfold.'[28] Trade slackened temporarily during the Reformation but after the Restoration of the Monarchy demand caught up again and surpassed all records.

Indian quilts were much in demand because their exotic painted designs in fast, bright colours were so different from the woven textile and monochrome prints available in Britain. Not only finished quilts were imported; palampores and lengths of chintz for a variety of costume and furnishing uses were also brought into Britain. These fabrics became the mainstay of a flourishing quiltmaking industry; they were wadded with wool instead of the cotton used in India, backed with woollen fabric and quilted in simple, allover designs.

THE
CASE
OF THE
Makers of QUILTS for BEDS only.

316

I. **T**HAT depriving the Quilt-Makers of the Liberty of ufing *Printed Callicoe Carpets*, will be a Detriment to the *Government*, as to the *Cuftoms* and *Duties*, and alfo to the *Woollen Manufactures* ; there being great Quantities of *Norwich*, *Kidderminfter*, *Kendal*, and other Stuffs, ufed for the Backfides of *Quilts* ; befides abundance of *Ordinary Wooll*, which muft otherwife be thrown away ; it being too fhort for *Spinning*, and fit for no other Ufe.

II. That the *Callicoes* ufed in making *Quilts*, are cut into fquare Pieces, and printed in Form of a *Carpet*, which renders them unfit for *Cloaths* or *Garments* of any kind : Neither can they be ufed in *Houfhold Furniture* any otherways but in *Quilts*, being only fit for that Purpofe.

III. That *Linnen Cloths* and *Woollen Stuffs*, are not proper for *Quilts*, the one being Cold and Heavy, and the *Woollen* will harbour Filth and Dirt, and be much of the fame kind as *Rugs* are ; and not being capable of being clean'd fo well as *Callicoe Carpets*, renders them altogether unfit for that Purpofe : For the whole Defign in having *Quilts* for Beds, is, to have them Light and Warm, and made of That which will clean often, and not harbour Filth and Dirt, as the *Rugs* ufed to do.

IV. Therefore, It is humbly prayed, That a *Claufe* may be inferted in the faid *Bill*, To preferve the Ufe and Wear of *Printed Callicoe Carpets* in *Quilts* for *Beds* only ; there being nothing fo proper for that Ufe : The fame being no-ways prejudicial to any of the *Manufactures* of this Kingdom, but rather an Encouragement ; and alfo imploys abundance of Poor in Working up the fame.

45. *Painted Indian chintz quilt quilted with allover pattern of concentric rectangles: eighteenth century (264 × 213 cm—104 × $83\frac{7}{8}$ in.)*

But towards the end of the seventeenth century, the industry came under threat – British textile manufacturers became increasingly concerned at the competition from India and lobbied for trade restrictions. Faced with this threat, the 'Quilt-Makers' issued the 'broadsheet' illustrated in fig. 44. This fascinating document reveals a great deal about the quiltmaking trade, not least the staggering quantity of quilts it must have produced. Yet only two known quilts which could have come from this source have survived: one is in Toronto Museum[29] and the other in the collection of the Victoria and Albert Museum (fig. 45).

What of the poor people of Britain – those at the lower levels of society? The East India Company clearly felt a need to broaden its trade by importing goods which might appeal to the lower end of the market. In a letter of 1683, we read that bed furnishings should be 'none too dear . . . you know only the poorest people in England lye without any curtains or vallances'.[30] But the evidence from wills and inventories, by now a legal requirement upon death for every adult in the land, suggests that the fashion for quilts and quilted garments made little impact on the lives of common people. In *Jacobean Household Inventories*, F. G. Emmison lists 166 inventories for the single year 1619. Of these lists, representing the property and effects of men and women from all but the very highest levels of society, only five include any mention of a quilt. And, of those, two quite clearly specify that the quilts were old and of little value: in the 'upper chamber' of the home of William Mason, tailor of St John, Bedford, was listed 'one old broken quilt 12d [5p] . . . one coverlet 13s 4d [67p]'[31] – an interesting comparison in value. In *Farm and Cottage Inventories in Mid Essex, 1635–1749*, an even sparser picture emerges of the use of quilts at this level of society. Not until 1690 does a quilt feature amongst the possessions of the humbler folk of Essex and even this is an 'old quilt'.[32] But in the will of William Rind of Horsely Park in Writtle (1691), the influence of fashion is seen: in his 'Parlour Chamber' (obviously his best chamber) is listed 'a painted callicoe quilt', and in the 'Pantry Chamber' a more serviceable 'gray searge quilt'.[33] These two wills, nevertheless, are the only two out of nearly 200 published in this volume, and representing the period 1635–1700, in which quilts are even mentioned.

So, by the close of the seventeenth century, quilts still had no significant place in the bed furnishings of common people. Free-standing beds were by now commonplace but only wealthy people had elaborate frameworks; most had a simple, solid framework which sometimes supported a tester or canopy from which a valance or curtain hung. Feather-bed mattresses had long since replaced straw palliasses and a typical list of bedding would include sheets, blankets and a coverlet or rug (*happing* in the North of England) for use as a top cover. Despite the growing affluence of the country, the gap between rich and poor was still a wide one and the fashionable trends of the rich made little impression on humbler folk.

EIGHTEENTH CENTURY

The fashion for quilts and quilted garments continued unabated into the first half of the eighteenth century – many of them professionally made or at least with the pattern professionally marked. In 1706, Lady Grisel Baillie records paying 5s (25p) for 'drawing Grisel's petticoat',[34] and in 1750, a pattern-drawer was paid 10s 6d (52p) for marking out a quilt pattern.[35] Since the task took him five days it was more likely for a corded quilt than a wadded one. Describing the Sturbridge Fair, near Cambridge, in the 1720s, Daniel Defoe records stalls 'taken up with upholsterer's ware, such as tickings, sackings, Kidderminster stuffs, blankets, rugs, quilts etc.'.[36] These quilts were probably British made, for Indian quilts, though still much sought after, were by now banned from import and unlikely to be on open sale.

It is clear from the now more numerous surviving examples that the fashionable style of wadded quilting already seen in the previous century continued through until at least the mid-eighteenth century. Expensive silks and satin continued to be used for wadded quilts and quilted clothing, though linen was used for flat and corded work (linen quilting became almost a separate branch of the craft). Wool was used to wad these silk and satin pieces and silk thread was most often used for quilting (see fig. 46). Costume items, however, far outnumber surviving quilts. When particular garments ceased to be fashionable they were either handed on to a servant or stored away, some to find their way eventually into public and private collections. Quilts, on the other hand, could still be found a practical use even when their style had ceased to be fashionable and most must eventually have worn out. It is

46. *Detail of cot-sized quilt (117 × 89 cm— 46 × 35 in.) in yellow satin with silk backing and wool filling; English: seventeenth century*

from surviving costume rather than quilts that eighteenth-century quilting styles and techniques can be most clearly seen.

Though a variety of costume garments were quilted, petticoats were especially popular, particularly in the first half of the eighteenth century. In fashionable silk and satin, they were wadded lightly with wool, and worn between the cut-away skirts of informal day dresses. It was a fashion universal throughout Britain, Europe and the American colonies. It was also a fashion which reached down through all social levels, though a new quilted petticoat was an expensive item to buy: in the early 1720s the price is given as £3 19s 2d (£3.91).[37] But prosperity was growing and those who could not afford to buy new clothes often obtained them second-hand. Quilted petticoats could be seen on girls and women at the lower level of society long after they had gone out of fashion amongst the middle and upper classes. Remembering his childhood in the late 1770s, Francis Place 'remembered the wives and daughters of the journeymen and shopkeepers of London in their leather stays and quilted camlet petticoats'.[38]

The close similarity in style and pattern between wadded quilts and petticoats is worth noting – it is a connection which reappears in the next century. Within these silk and satin pieces, some at least made professionally, so many of the common patterns of traditional quilting can be found – stylized leaf and flower patterns, *feathers*, *roses*, *scrolls*, *waves*, *shells*, *wineglasses*, geometrically divided borders – together with the baskets of flowers and cornucopias which echo floral styles of embroidery. And the hand of the amateur can clearly be seen in the naïve and imprecise way some patterns are drawn as quilting became more home-based. As women with fewer financial resources strove to keep up with the fashions of the time, they not only did their own quilting but designed and marked their own patterns.

47. *Detail of
eighteenth–century
quilted silk petticoat*

It was in the eighteenth century that quilts, too, began to move down the social scale. From around 1700 onwards, they begin to figure with greater frequency in the wills of ordinary people, though they were still far from a common bed covering in most homes up to the mid-eighteenth century. After that, the picture is obscured, for a change in law made it unnecessary for such comprehensive inventories of a deceased's property to be made.

Where quilts were to be found in ordinary houses and cottages, they were usually confined to the 'best' room. The 'Best Chamber' of Joseph Goodman, miller of Writtle, Essex, who died in 1730, contained 'blankets and quilt' but no such luxuries were to be found in his other rooms.[39] The price of quilts seems to have fallen somewhat from the inflated prices of the previous years if the values quoted in the wills of two inhabitants of Newcastle upon Tyne can be taken as a firm indication. In 1700, widow Hankin left a 'craddle quilt valued at 2s 6d [12½p] and upholsterer Hill left a quilt valued at 5s [25p]'.[40] Of course, these values are for quilts which had been in use but it is unlikely that widow Hankin, at least, acquired her quilt second-hand, for she was a lady of some means. Perhaps the price of quilts was now much more within reach of increasingly prosperous tradespeople.

Little is known, unfortunately, of the types of quilts in use in modest homes until much later in the eighteenth century when patchwork quilts became more commonplace. It is often assumed that wholecloth quilts of workaday fabrics, like homespun wool or linsey-woolsey, were made in farms and cottages for domestic use. It is not an unreasonable assumption, for one 'searge quilt' is recorded from the late seventeenth century,[41] and a very few linsey-woolsey and homespun quilts, dated around 1800, have survived (figs. 55 and 72). Domestic quilting undoubtedly increased throughout the eighteenth century. By the end of the century, making quilts was a common activity amongst ordinary folk, but the precise nature of the move from country house and manor to farm and cottage can only be surmised. Perhaps the patterns and skills learnt initially in making quilts and petticoats for their masters were eventually taken and used, by common folk, for their own purposes.

48. *Reverse side of quilt of pieced embroidered linen (dated 1690) quilted at a later date with a bordered quilting design to which new borders have been subsequently added on three sides.*

But as the vogue for quiltmaking moved into farms and cottages, it rapidly declined amongst the fashionable upper and middle classes. Instead, unquilted patchwork covers pieced initially from Indian chintz replaced quilts as fashionable bed covers in the second half of the eighteenth century. Patchwork had already been used for quilts, as the widely described and illustrated Levens Hall quilt[42] of 1708, and a once beautiful but now sadly tattered silk quilt (*c.*1750) in Exeter Museum, both show. But in the second half of the eighteenth century, it was used more for coverlets than quilts by the leisured ladies of the upper and middle classes – the beginnings of the division in Britain between patchwork and quilting which was to leave its mark for the next century and a half.

One of the initial factors which helped to popularize patchwork was its use for making the most of much-prized Indian chintz. This economical attitude extended to making the most of other precious fabrics too. The top-side of the quilt in fig. 48 is of pieced sections of embroidered linen, probably re-used bed hangings dating from 1690. Even the quilt made from the re-used hangings has been cut up and recycled. The original centre section (marked by a precise and skilful hand) and one border have been kept but, on the other three sides, borders have been added which are more reminiscent of a style of quilting belonging to the

49. *Medallion quilt of cotton prints with centre panel of print produced to commemorate the Golden Jubilee of George III in 1810, and quilted with allover wave quilting; North Country: c.1810–20 (259 × 259 cm—102 × 102 in.)*

late eighteenth or early nineteenth century. The whole of the quilt is a fascinating collection of decorative needlecraft styles which probably span about a hundred years. The quilt in fig. 68 shows a similar economy. Its top cover is pieced from several sections of green silk, the nature of the piecing more apparent in the photograph than in reality. Despite the pieced nature of the cover, this is still a fine quilt meticulously drawn and worked in a style so similar to quilted petticoats of the same period.

The changing fortunes of the textile industry had a considerable effect on quiltmaking and the use of quilts in eighteenth-century Britain. The early years of the century saw the first decline in the Indian textile trade. Despite their pleas (fig. 44), the small band of quiltmakers had little chance against the large and effective lobby of British textile manufacturers and, in 1700 and 1701, two Acts of Parliament were passed, first imposing a 15 per cent import duty and then totally prohibiting the import of all Indian textiles for home consumption. But the legislation was ineffective because chintz could still be imported for re-export and this loophole allowed unscrupulous merchants to evade the legislation. In 1720, a further Act was introduced to ban the use and wear of imported chintz and, though only partly successful, it signalled a decline in the Indian trade from which it never fully recovered. Although restrictions were relaxed in the second half of the century, textile manufacturing and printing in Britain, under pressure from Indian competition, had advanced technologically and were well able to compete with renewed imports.

What became of the quiltmakers who so eloquently pleaded their case is not known but it seems likely that prohibition on the import of chintz began the decline of quilting as a professional trade. When, in the second half of the century, quilted clothing declined in popularity, their demise was probably complete.

The decline of the Indian trade in such an enforced manner left another legacy. Far from preventing the use of chintz, the Act of 1720 made it even more desirable – prohibition had its romantic appeal! Pieces of chintz were hoarded and some were eventually incorporated into quilts and coverlets in the later years of the century. When trade resumed, Indian chintz was still eagerly sought but chintz-style fabrics could now be produced in Britain as textile-printing techniques improved.

Towards the end of the eighteenth century another change of far-reaching significance took place. The Industrial Revolution gathered pace and the manufacture of cotton goods rapidly expanded after 1760, particularly in Lancashire. Within a few years, attractive cotton prints were available to the mass of British people through both retailers and travelling salesmen who peddled the home-produced cotton fabrics around the country. Bought initially for dress-use, leftovers or old scraps were pieced into patchwork covers (especially medallion ones), then backed with cotton or linen, filled with wool, and made into inexpensive and pretty quilts for farmhouse or cottage.

So a century which began with elaborate, often professionally made quilts, or imported Indian ones gracing the beds of wealthy and upper-class families, ended with unpretentious, domestically made wadded quilts used as decorative bed covers in humble homes throughout much of Britain. Changes in fashion, industry and society in eighteenth-century Britain had a profound effect upon quilting both in Britain and in America which quickly followed the changes in fashion taking place on the eastern side of the Atlantic.

NINETEENTH CENTURY

The nineteenth century became the age of the cotton quilt for, as the expansion of the textile industry in Lancashire gathered pace, new and inexpensive cottons reached the market. By 1800, too, the move down the social scale was virtually complete as quilting became a firmly established part of traditional culture in parts of rural Britain.

Most evidence for the types of traditional quilts made in nineteenth-century Britain comes from surviving and recorded examples and from oral-history sources. Recorded history or contemporary literary sources tell us little for, in moving down the social scale and particularly into the hands of women, quilting ceased to be worthy of comment by historians and writers of the time. Only recently has popular history and popular culture obtained any academic credibility. Only recently, too, has oral history (the recording from surviving individuals of their memories of a bygone age) achieved respectability as a recording method, so even oral-history sources can tell us little before 1850.

How typical surviving and recorded quilts are of those that were made throughout the nineteenth century is a difficult question. The survival of an individual quilt can be the result of many chance factors but, in general, 'best' quilts were more likely to be well looked after and handed on than those in everyday use: so a biased sample is more than likely what we now see. Nevertheless, from those quilts which have survived or been recorded, it is possible to follow changing trends in style and pattern through the century.

50. Block patchwork quilt in Feathered Star *pattern, in cottons, quilted with an allover pattern of* daisy flowers *and* square-diamonds *infill; North Country: c.1890 (204 × 204 cm—80 × 80 in.)*

In the early years of the nineteenth century, patchwork quilts predominate over other types, with top covers pieced in multicoloured cottons, though often backed with linen. Fabrics were of pastel or what now appear muted, even drab, tones, but many must have faded or altered from their original colour. And, of the patchwork quilts, central medallion designs were much the most popular in all regions in the first half of the century. Up to about 1830, specially printed chintz blocks (some commemorative) were often used for the centres of medallion quilts (fig. 49) with the patchwork pieces in a variety of prints including large-scale floral 'chintz-style' prints and even chinoiserie ones. As the century progressed and other printed fabrics became more widely available, the small-scale sprigged and floral prints characteristic of Victorian Britain were incorporated into either multicoloured medallion, or two-colour block patchwork or strip quilts.

Appliquéd quilts, with simple motif patterns cut from multicoloured cottons, were popular in the first half of the nineteenth century but appliqué was little used (except in the North Pennine Dales) after 1850. The *broderie perse* type of appliqué was also worked, but rarely in humble homes – like 'paper patchwork' in the eighteenth century, it was a more 'bourgeois' type of needlework.

Wholecloth quilts were of two extremes in the early part of the nineteenth century. On the one hand, all-white cotton or linen quilts beautifully stitched in elaborate patterns were

1. Medallion quilt with chintz and patchwork panels in the centre of a strippy ground and quilted with an allover square-diamond *pattern; English: c.1820—40 (262 x 226 cm — 103 x 89 in.)*

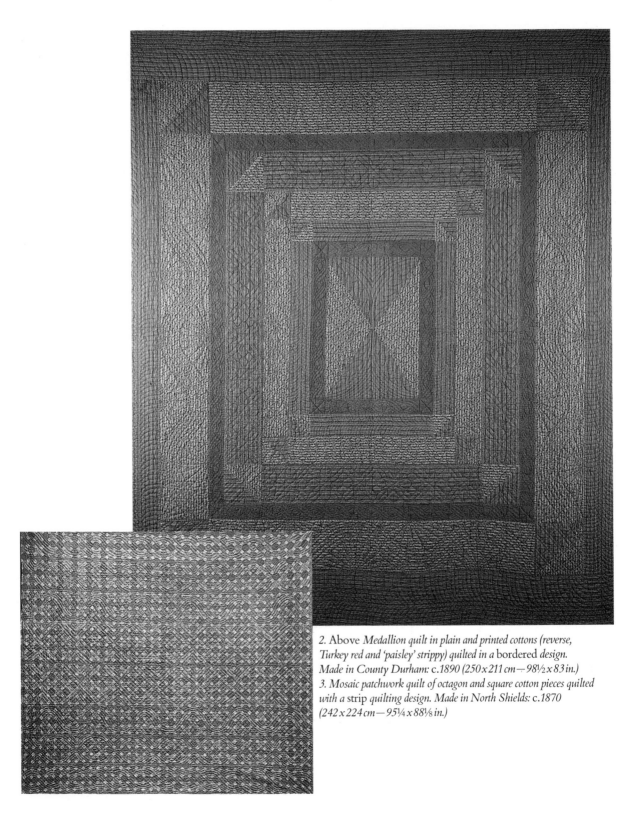

2. Above *Medallion quilt in plain and printed cottons (reverse,
Turkey red and 'paisley' strippy) quilted in a bordered design.
Made in County Durham: c.1890 (250 x 211 cm — 98½ x 83 in.)*
3. *Mosaic patchwork quilt of octagon and square cotton pieces quilted
with a strip quilting design. Made in North Shields: c.1870
(242 x 224 cm — 95¼ x 88⅛ in.)*

4. *Patchwork quilt in cotton rectangles quilted with a* strip *quilting design; North Country: late nineteenth century/early twentieth century (213 x 177 cm — 83⅞ x 69⅝ in.)*

5. Above *Appliquéd block quilt with motifs applied to a white cotton patched background and quilted with an allover bellows pattern. Made as a marriage quilt by Charlotte McCartney (1858–1954) of Washington, Co. Durham, who subsequently never married: 1880 (238 x 198 cm — 93¾ x 78 in.)*

6. *Medallion quilt with* Princess Feather *appliquéd centre and quilted with a bordered quilting design. Made by a member of the Wood family, West Woodburn, Northumberland: 1870–90 (241 x 238 cm — 94⅞ x 93¾ in.)*

7. Strippy quilt in cotton sateen quilted with a strip *quilting design, North Country: early twentieth century (239 x 218 cm — 94 x 95⅞ in.)*

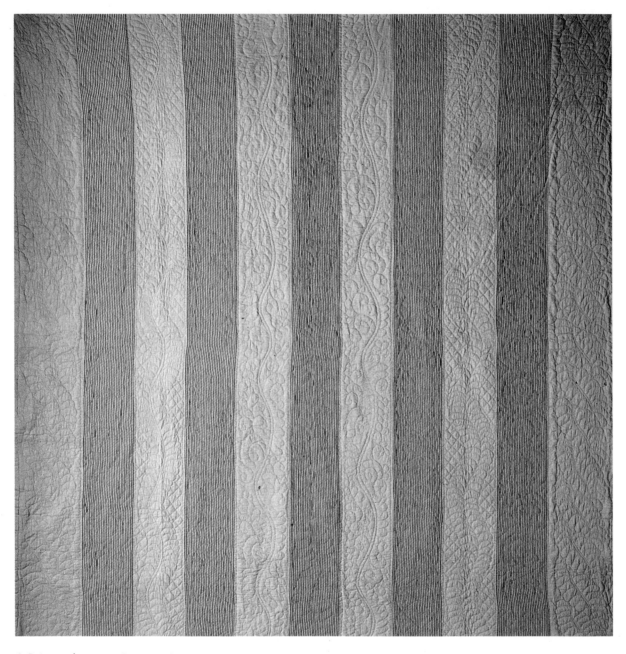

8. Strippy quilt in cottons (reverse, pink cotton) quilted with a strip quilting design. Made by Mrs Harriet Walton of Frosterley, Co. Durham: c.1933 (208 x 194 cm — 81⅛ x 76⅜ in.)

9. Centre detail with lovers' knot *central motif from an all-white wholecloth quilt designed in Allendale and quilted by Mrs Louise Rutherford of Rothbury, Northumberland: c.1910*

10. Medallion star *quilt in cotton sateen pieced and quilted in the style of Elizabeth Sanderson; North Country: c.1930 (210 x 210 cm — 82⅝ x 82⅝ in.)*

made for 'best' use whilst, on the other, wholecloth quilts of linsey-woolsey, homespun, or manufactured wool were worked for everyday use. But as bought cotton fabrics became even cheaper in the second half of the century, cotton sateen was increasingly used. These wholecloth sateen quilts, and strippy quilts, replaced patchwork ones as the common quilt types of the post-1850 period.

The strippy quilt probably made its first appearance in the nineteenth century but it is hard to say precisely when or where. The earliest recorded strippy quilt (in the Manx Museum) is dated at around 1840 but the great majority of surviving quilts of this type were made after 1860. The vogue for Turkey red and white quilts was also a nineteenth-century fashion. Though most surviving red and white quilts are from the second half of the century, they were made earlier, for a fast red vegetable dye had long been available. The fashion was given a further boost, however, with the discovery of chemical dyes by Perkins in 1856, which led to a revolution in dyeing processes.

The post-1850 period also saw the influence of the now strong and independent American tradition of quiltmaking on British patchwork and appliquéd quilts and coverlets, especially in the North Pennine Dales. Though some might disagree, my own feeling is that patterns like *Feathered Star*, *Princess Feather*, and the post-1850 vogue for red, green and white quilts owe more to the American tradition than to the British one. There was more vitality and imagination in American quiltmaking at this time and therefore more likelihood of new designs and patterns emerging.

The designs quilted on to these nineteenth-century quilts varied with the nature of the covers and, no doubt, the intended use of the quilt. 'Best' quilts were often quilted with *bordered* designs whatever the covers, though some carefully worked patchwork and appliquéd quilts were quilted with simple *allover* designs. The *bordered* designs worked in the early part of the century were clearly more elaborate and closely worked than those produced later. A gradual 'loosening' of *bordered* designs is noticeable as the century progresses – a trend which persisted through the twentieth century (except for the 1930s). The years 1800–50 represent the high point of traditional quilting in Britain, as a whole, but the years of the preceding centuries must have laid the foundations for the tradition and for the precise and confident designs produced, by women and men, in the farms and cottages of rural Britain.

As well as a general 'loosening' of design, the second half of the nineteenth century saw a clear divergence of style in the two regions of Britain where quilting survived throughout the century – the North of England, most particularly the North-East counties, and Wales. Particular patterns became clearly identified as belonging to one or other of the regions: *hearts* and *spiral* patterns were recognizably 'Welsh', *feathers* and *roses* became 'North Country' patterns. In other ways, however, Welsh quilting stayed closer to its eighteenth-century roots – *bordered* designs with a number of clearly delineated and geometrically divided borders were still the most commonly worked design on all but the most 'everyday', roughly worked quilts.

In the North of England quilting design evolved markedly. Two clear changes are evident in the second half of the nineteenth century. The first was the development of *strip* quilting designs; easy to work and easy to quilt, they became very popular, especially for strippy quilts. The second change seems clearly identified with a single individual. George Gardiner of Allendale, in the North Pennine Dales, was the first of the noted quilt designers of Allendale and Weardale. It was the quilt designers who were largely responsible for the intricate, flowing style now so closely associated with North Country quilts. The *bordered* designs they marked for customers showed a movement away from the old-style designs:

elaborate, curvilinear patterns for centres, corners and borders with scrolling infill were typical. The pattern elements were not contained but allowed to merge or flow together and into the central field invariably filled with *square-diamonds* (see figs. 58 and 59). Inevitably, the style was copied by other quilters in the region.

The nineteenth century was also the age of the economy quilt; saving fabric scraps for a patchwork quilt was practical and appealed to the Victorian value of thrift. Towards the end of the century, cotton fabrics were cheap to buy and a wholecloth or strippy cover could be run up very quickly by machine. Adding new covers, or ones pieced from scraps, to a worn blanket and turning it into a quilt gave it a new lease of life, for wool blankets were expensive items to buy and not lightly discarded. '. . . they had a woollen blanket that was getting too thin to be of much use on the bed. They would have new material on the top, the almost worn out blanket in the centre and then a pair of curtains unpicked and washed to back it with', remembers one Northumbrian lady.[43]

In Wales, not only old blankets but all kinds of discarded fabrics were used to fill quilts. Many of these 'economy' quilts were poorly worked with inaccurately drawn designs and rough stitching, but not all – some carefully worked *bordered* designs were quilted on a blanket filling.

Although quilting in nineteenth-century Britain was home-based, it was not solely in the hands of the amateur. At every stage in the century there were professionals who were paid for some aspect of the craft. Itinerant quilters are recorded from Wales and the North of England. Some spent only part of the year travelling around, but one Welsh quilter apparently spent all her time moving between farms and cottages: 'If I rightly remember she did not have a home; it was going about like that she was'.[44] Others made quilts as only one of several bread-winning activities, like Hannah Emmerson of Weardale, whose husband (a miner and small farmer) died in his fifties leaving her a mortgaged farm. Refusing to sell the farm, Hannah carried on alone. 'On top of that she charred, made beautiful quilts by the dim light of the candles, brought new lives into the world in a wide area and did the necessary duties when life expired.'[45]

In the mining villages of Northumberland and Durham, quilt 'clubs' (see pages 122–5) provided much-needed income for women whose domestic circumstances forced them to become at least partial bread-winners. Established in the late nineteenth century, quilt 'clubs' also operated in the mining valleys of South Wales,[46] although specific instances have not been recorded.

Only in the North of England did anyone earn a living from designing quilts. The designers or 'quilt stampers' of Allendale and Weardale became so well known for the quality of their designs that they were never short of work. Elizabeth Sanderson's niece (see pages 117–18) remembers the pile of fabric in the farmhouse living-room, waiting to be worked, when she went for the occasional holiday as a child, in the early years of this century. But no one ever became fat on the proceeds of quilting – even Joe Hedley, of Northumberland, renowned for his quilts and thought to have been murdered for the money he supposedly made from them, died on parish relief.

Some of the professional quilters (except the quilt 'club' quilters) made not only quilts but quilted petticoats, for these again became fashionable amongst country women in the second half of the nineteenth century. It may even be that, in country districts, quilted petticoats were worn right through the nineteenth century for in a dialect poem of the 1830s Thomas Wilson wrote of his 'bonny Sal':

> Her twilted petticoat so fine
> Frae side to side a fathom stritchin
> A stitch'd wi' many a fancied line
> Wad stan' itsel', and was bewitchin.[47]

The later nineteenth-century petticoats were quite different from their eighteenth-century counterparts, however, and were made for warmth rather than decoration. They were worn by women whose working lives were spent as much outdoors as in, those in fishing and agricultural communities where women played an important part in the economic life of the community. In some parts of the North of England, these petticoats were worn until the early years of the twentieth century. In serviceable woollen fabrics, often black, the petticoats were wadded with wool or cotton and quilted with simple patterns, sometimes only on the lower part. Quilted petticoats of this type have survived from Wales, Yorkshire and the North-East of England: they have also been recorded in the West of England. One Northumberland lady remembers her mother wearing a black quilted petticoat – and the reason why: 'They were lovely and warm when you had to travel in an open cart.'[48]

In nineteenth-century Britain, quilting was not always a solitary occupation – families quilted together round a frame (fig. 54). However, in the North Pennine Dales, quilting parties were a social occasion akin to the American 'quilting bee'. Though less well known and only rarely documented, they were nevertheless a flourishing part of communal life. In the North of England too, church and chapel groups met regularly for sewing meetings to raise funds: making quilts was a regular activity in these groups.

Though the first half of the nineteenth century produced some of the best of traditional British quilts, the vitality and quality of quilting design was not to last. Society was changing rapidly in the wake of the Industrial Revolution and the novelty of new, machine-made bed covers made quilts seem very much 'second-best'. The Marcella quilt (so named from Marseilles where it was first made) was a particular threat to the hand-stitched quilt for the designs, woven on a Jacquard-type loom, were a close imitation of *bordered* quilting designs. The move from country to town also gathered pace through the century, and as urbanization increased so life-styles and communities changed. In the West of England, quilts were rarely made after 1900 and, since this is only known from the work of Elizabeth Hake in the 1930s, it is a reasonable assumption that the same might have happened in other rural counties where quilting has so far been unrecorded.

TWENTIETH CENTURY

In the early years of the twentieth century, quilting survived as an active traditional craft only in South Wales and the North of England. Even in these two regions it was now under threat. Commercially made bedspreads and eiderdowns could be bought from shops and were relatively inexpensive. Eiderdowns were particularly fashionable and had been so in more affluent homes from the later years of the nineteenth century. As their popularity increased, so hand-sewn traditional quilts declined in use. By the 1920s, quilts were regarded as old-fashioned in areas where, ten years previously, they had been the common top bed covering in working-class homes.

Fashion and taste were not the only enemies; the outbreak of war in 1914 dealt traditional quilting another blow. Fabrics became difficult to obtain and, by the time war ended in 1918, the role of women in society was changing as they began to seek, and to find, working roles outside the home. Even in rural areas, like the North Pennine Dales, where quiltmaking had been an important part of traditional culture, decline set in and fewer young girls were taught by their mothers to quilt. Only in the areas where quilt 'clubs' and church quilting groups were an established part of social practice was traditional quilting revived to any extent after the First World War. The 'clubs' and church groups in North-East England continued to produce strippy and wholecloth quilts through the 1920s and into the 1930s; indeed, the war memorial in Amble, Northumberland, was partly financed by the efforts of a quilting group.

In those early post-war years, quilting received its first boost from an organizational source. The newly formed Women's Institute took an active interest in all forms of needlework, including traditional quilting. One Northumberland lady remembers her local Women's Institute group meeting once a week to make quilts: 'these quilts were very often used for exhibition or for fund raising . . . The price they would bring in would be according to the work and the quality. It would be from £4 10s (£4.50) in those days (early 1920s) and £5 to £10 if it was a really good one.'[49]

In the late 1920s, another organization began to take an interest in quilting – the Rural Industries Bureau (RIB), the forerunner of the Council of Small Industries in Rural Areas (CoSIRA). The aims and operation of the quilting scheme, run for ten years (1929–39), are well summed up in the Report published by the Rural Industries Bureau on its work during 1929–36.

This section of the advisory work of the Bureau, in some respects the most completely successful, began as an effort to give assistance in what were then known as the 'distressed areas'. A survey of the South Wales and Durham areas revealed the fact that wives of miners were producing for their homes quilts which in technique and pattern were true to a tradition dating back 300 years. It was obvious that given good material in place of the worn-out blankets and cheap cotton covers which customarily were used, the unique character of the work and rare qualities of the design would give to the quilts a commercial value, and that little more than organisation was needed for success to be assured. Advisory help in the form demanded by the blacksmith, potter and wood-worker was not called for, but the cost of experimental work had to be met, and this the Bureau was not constituted to give. A grant of £250, however, was obtained from the Pilgrim Trust and was used to cover the cost of establishing classes for the training of young women by the older quilters, and for the provision of materials of the quality demanded by the trade.

Success was immediate, and during the period of greatest distress whole families were saved from utter destitution by the income derived from the sale of the work of their women-folk.

Two factors in this success were the high aesthetic quality of the designs, and the provision of a capital sum for which no return was demanded. The latter is unique in the work of the Bureau, and its significance cannot be ignored. The Bureau is debarred by its constitution from incurring trading risks, and agents were appointed to conduct sales at ordinary commercial rates, an officer of the Bureau being responsible for maintaining contact with the workers, controlling rates of pay, the provision of material and supervision of training classes.

Exhibitions were organised and many private houses were generously lent for this purpose. Sales in the first three years were upwards of £10,000 and that these were by no means compassionate sales is shown by the continuance of sales at the high yearly average of £3,750.

The organisation which was established as an emergency expedient has been found adequate, and there is no reason why the production and sale of these quilts should not remain a permanent industry in these two mining areas.[50]

The quilts produced under the Rural Industries Bureau scheme were all wholecloth quilts, of silk or a good quality cotton sateen or poplin, wool-filled and quilted with intricate *bordered* designs. Smaller items were also made – cushions, jackets, dressing gowns and baby's matinée sets (fig. 51). The standard of design and workmanship, especially of the Welsh quilts, was very high and rivals some of the best early nineteenth-century work. It had to be good to meet the demand of the market – it was undoubtedly market pressure which led to such an improvement in quilting. 'It is only by emphasising the necessity for the best workmanship and for the preservation of the traditional patterns as the main feature of the quilts, that the problem of marketing has been dealt with successfully.'[51]

51. Prices charged for quilted items produced under the Rural Industries Bureau scheme in the 1930s and sold at the Little Gallery, London

PRICES OF QUILTED WORK

PRICES vary according to the amount of work in the pattern and the materials used. The average prices per square foot, for large quilts, when there is no waste of material, are:

Sateen or fine cotton   ..   ..   3/8 per square foot
Fine cotton poplin ..   ..   ..   4/- per square foot
Shanghai silk   ..   ..   ..   6/- per square foot

———————

Estimates can be given for sizes and materials required. The following are specimen prices for standard sizes:

Silk Dressing Gowns, quilted all over, from ..   £8 8 0
Silk Dressing Jackets, quilted all over..   ..   £5 10 0
Silk Cushions, down filled, from £1 18 6

Cot Quilts (about 3 ft. × 2 ft.):

Sateen or fine cotton, from £1 5 0
Poplin £1 8 6
Silk £2 2 0

Quilts for single beds:

Eiderdown size (about 5 ft. × 4 ft.)
Sateen or fine cotton £3 15 0
Silk £5 10 0
Counterpane size (about 6 ft. × 7 ft.)
Sateen or fine cotton £7 7 0
Poplin £8 8 0
Silk £11 11 0

The success of the scheme was due, in no small part, to the seemingly tireless efforts and enthusiasm of Mavis Fitzrandolph, the Bureau officer responsible. Her insistence upon high standards of design and workmanship, the use of good-quality materials and the close liaison she kept – both with the quilters and with the galleries which marketed the work – were important factors. Muriel Rose of the Little Gallery in London, one of the galleries through which the quilts were sold, was also enthusiastically involved – but she too 'had no time for better than second rate but not first class work'.[52] So it was not mere altruism which brought success but also the intrinsic beauty and quality of the work produced, under guiding hands, by the 'quilt wives'. A particular achievement was the large order secured from Claridge's Hotel, London, in the early 1930s for quilts and pillow slips for their new wing.

Quilt wives in South Wales and County Durham have been chosen to make bed coverlets and daytime pillow-slips for the bedrooms in the new wing of Claridge's Hotel. The most beautiful of the traditional patterns have been used, and some fifty women have taken part in the work, which has been carried out very quickly. Some of the co-operative quilting groups in South Wales are able to finish a pair of large quilts, with pillow covers to match, within a week, and many of the County Durham quilters have worked in pairs at the frames to complete the orders in time.[53]

Sadly, the scheme was brought to an abrupt end by the outbreak of the Second World War in 1939. Textile manufacture was cut back and geared to the war effort and this, together with rationing, made it impossible to supply quilters with materials. But the Rural Industries Bureau had succeeded in creating a new type of professional quilter – one who worked for a luxury market beyond her own locality.

The outbreak of war was also the final blow to the few remaining quilters still running quilt 'clubs' in North-East England. Many were in Northumberland, for Durham quilters were involved in the Rural Industries Bureau scheme, but their fortunes had been declining for some years. Fewer local people wanted quilts at this 'down-market' end of the business. When the Second World War ended, their 'clubs' never revived, though some of the quilters took the occasional private commission. A handful of church groups, mostly around Sunderland, did restart – one is still in existence. But these group quilters had no design skills – most sent their quilt tops to the quilt designers, now only in Allendale, whose services remained in demand. It is a practice that survives to this day.

Of these women who had actively quilted before 1939, either for themselves or for the Rural Industries Bureau scheme, very few began quiltmaking again in the late 1940s. In the 1950s, some took up teaching under the auspices of Local Education Authorities. Adult Education classes for quilting were established in Wales and North-East England but most were short-lived and the pupil who became an active quiltmaker was an extreme rarity. When in the 1970s the revival of interest in quiltmaking began in earnest, there were just two active teachers left – one in South Wales (Kate Lewis) and one in Durham (Amy Emms). They provided the most fragile of links between the old oral tradition and the new 'revival'.

The 'quilt revival' in Britain, however, was largely influenced from North America. With a more affluent and mobile society, visits to the USA and Canada brought women, in particular, into close contact with the American tradition of quiltmaking. Fired with enthusiasm for the colours and patterns of American quilts, they returned home to continue a new-found interest and to pass it on to others. Women's magazines began to publish articles on patchwork, quilting and appliqué and these reached an even wider audience. Books, exhibitions and television programmes appeared and eventually in 1978, the Quilters' Guild of Great Britain was formed. Thus the informal network at first established became a formal one based on a national guild providing a communication link for all quiltmakers, traditional and contemporary, throughout Great Britain.

But the inspiration and style of much quiltmaking today is still more closely linked to the American tradition than to the British one. The bright and varied patchwork and appliquéd designs of American quilts are visually striking and stimulating and, since the quiltmaking tradition survived into the twentieth century in greater strength North America than it did in Britain, there was a more obvious base on which the 'quilt revival' could build. However, as interest, expertise and knowledge have grown so too has a renewed interest in the British tradition. With it has come the recognition that this tradition encompasses a range of patchwork and quilting designs whose roots go back hundreds of years but whose branches will, it is hoped, continue to bear fruit.

6 Social and Regional Influences

There was an old neighbour who used to come in. She'd say 'I've tellt wor Geordie ah wanted to come alang and help Lizzie wi'ya quilt'. And she never put a stitch in. But she had that excuse to get out for an hour or two you see. Husbands were very exacting in those days!
Old Northumberland quilter (1978)[1]

The previous chapter has charted the course that quilting in general and quiltmaking in particular have taken since their first introduction into Britain. It was a progress, I believe, not just through time but through the various levels of British society – what began as a form of adornment for the rich and powerful became a part of traditional culture amongst the peasant and working-class communities of Britain. Why and how did this happen? And, once established as part of vernacular culture, why did traditional quilting survive into twentieth-century Britain in only isolated pockets?

One potent force at work in a class-divided society such as Britain is the pressure to 'better oneself' – to move up the social scale. Domestic possessions have always been seen as important social indicators. It seems likely that the possession of quilts became a typical manifestation of this pressure to attain a better class position, by imitating the ways of wealthier folk or those perceived to be of a higher social standing. From the sixteenth century onwards, the rapidly growing mercantile class sought to imitate and aspire to the life-styles of the aristocracy. If a rich and ornate quilt adorned the bed of a noble lord, why should the prosperous and confident merchant not also aquire such a lavish piece of bed furnishing? As country houses themselves passed from the hands of the aristocracy and gentry to successful merchants, they needed to be furnished in appropriate and fashionable style. A typical list of bedding for a mid-eighteenth-century country house is shown in fig. 52 and from this interesting document[2] the role of the quilts in such a house can be seen. But, by the time of this inventory (1788), the fashion for quilts was already declining and quilts, albeit second-best ones, were used as much in servants' rooms as in other bedrooms.

From about 1600 to 1750 quilts and quilted clothes were fashionable amongst the rich and powerful. But, though worn or used by the upper and middle classes, many were probably made either professionally, by craftsmen, or domestically, by servants. So the necessary design and needlecraft skills were possessed by the lower classes though they seem not to have used them initially for themselves: if a servant or a peasant possessed a quilt, it was more than likely as a 'hand-down'.

The eighteenth century, however, was a period when the use of quilts moved further down the social scale. In the second half of the century, quilts seem to have been commonly owned, and made, in rural farms and cottages. Again, social betterment was a likely pressure. But as quilts moved into farms and cottages they moved out of the country house and manor, or at least 'downstairs' into servants' rooms. Which move was cause and which

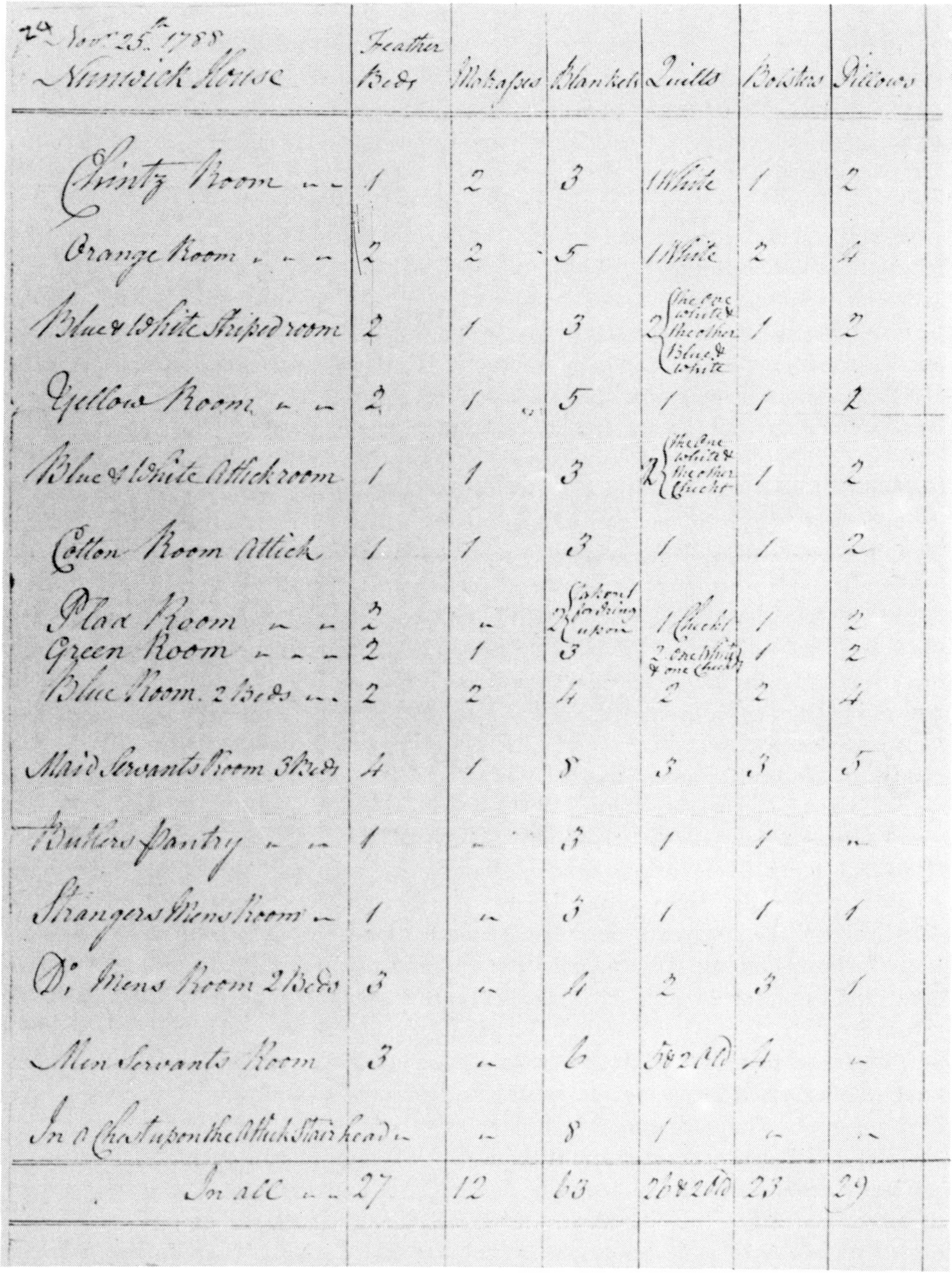

2ᵈ Novʳ 25ᵗʰ 1788
Nunwick House

	Feather Beds	Mattrasses	Blankets	Quilts	Bolsters	Pillows
Chintz Room	1	2	3	1 White	1	2
Orange Room	2	2	5	1 White	2	4
Blue & White Striped room	2	1	3	2 {the one white & the other Blue & White}	1	2
Yellow Room	2	1	5	1	1	2
Blue & White Attick room	1	1	3	2 {the one white & the other Chintz}	1	2
Cotton Room Attick	1	1	3	1	1	2
Flax Room	3	..	{Colourd Bedding upon}	1 Chintz	1	2
Green Room	2	1	3	2 one White & one Chintz	1	2
Blue Room. 2 Beds	2	2	4	2	2	4
Maid Servants Room 3 Beds	4	1	8	3	3	5
Butlers Pantry	1	..	3	1	1	..
Strangers Mens Room	1	..	3	1	1	1
Dᵒ Mens Room 2 Beds	3	..	4	2	3	1
Men Servants Room	3	..	6	5 & 2 old 4	..
In a Chest upon the Attick Stair head		..	8	1	..	..
In all	27	12	63	26 & 2 old	23	29

52. Inventory of beds
and bedding, Nunwick
House,
Northumberland

effect is an open question. Was quilting taken up, domestically, by the peasant class only *after* it had been abandoned by the upper and middle classes? Or was quilting abandoned in country house and manor *because* it became associated with the lower classes? Perhaps future work will shed some light on these questions. It may be that, for a period in the eighteenth century, quilts were made simultaneously at different levels of society. Only the fabrics used would have differed, with silks, satins and Indian chintz favoured by the wealthy, and homespun or the newly manufactured cottons used by the lower classes. By the close of the eighteenth century, however, quilting seems to have become firmly established as a part of traditional culture, i.e. the culture of the common people in Britain.

In the first half of the nineteenth century, traditional quilting flourished in many rural parts of Britain. With inexpensive materials available, it became a customary and popular activity and few brides went to the altar without at least one quilt in their 'bottom drawer'. But the nineteenth century was also a period of social upheaval. As rural workers moved to the new urban and industrial areas created in the wake of the Industrial Revolution, they took their oral traditions and skills with them. In some parts, especially the mining districts of South Wales and North-East England, traditional quilting was adapted to an economic and social role within the community with the establishment of quilt 'clubs'. Here it survived in some strength into the twentieth century. It also survived in rural areas remote from metropolitan influence, where traditions have always lingered, for example in the North Pennine Dales and South-West Wales. But elsewhere the traditional ways of rural Britain did not always find a place in its industrial counterpart.

Where quilting survived into the twentieth century, it was firmly associated with a rural or industrial working class. But when organizations like the Women's Institute and the Rural Industries Bureau began to take an interest, the main push came from a group of educated, middle-class women. At first, the concern was to preserve and encourage a dying traditional craft but, with the Depression of the 1930s, a more urgent need was perceived to create a market for quilting. With the Rural Industries Bureau scheme (see pages 100–102) the wheel came full circle, with quilts once again being made by professional quilters from the lower classes for use by upper- and middle-class customers – as had been the case over 200 years earlier.

This social categorization of quilting has left its mark. Once firmly established as part of *traditional* culture in Britain, quilting was largely abandoned by the upper and middle classes. It became a proletarian rather than a bourgeois activity and, as such, was subject to a social down-grading – a characteristic of the paternalism of British society which led traditional forms of culture to be judged as 'lower' than the 'higher' classical culture popularized by the bourgeoisie. The extraordinary strength of bourgeois culture, particularly in the nineteenth century, affected working-class culture in many ways, not least traditional quilting. It was judged from a position of superiority to be a 'lower' form of needlework and therefore not suitable either for the leisured ladies of the upper and middle classes or to be taught in schools. Embroidery and patchwork were acceptable: quilting was not! This social attitude to quilting manifested itself in other ways; because traditional quilts were so categorized they were not treasured or collected, so comparatively few examples have survived of the thousands which must have been made.

Once absorbed into traditional culture, quilting was moulded and adapted to fit the needs and life-styles of the common people of Britain. They took the basic designs and patterns, previously used on quilts and petticoats made for affluent society, and adapted them for use on homespun, linen and cotton quilts. So few wadded quilts have survived from the transition period in the eighteenth century that it is difficult – and dangerous – to make too many general assumptions about the direction in which style and pattern evolved. But some common elements can be seen. *Bordered* quilting designs predominated amongst 'best' quilts, often elaborate and closely worked. Baskets or vases of leaves and flowers were common centre and corner motifs: borders were geometrically divided more often than not. A single border was rare; usually two or three borders surrounded the central field.

At what point this basic style evolved in different regional directions is difficult to determine but it seems that, by the second half of the nineteenth century, a conscious regional 'stamp' had developed on quilts produced in Wales and the North of England. Elizabeth Hake considers that the quilts made in the West of England show a more 'naturalistic' style with patterns based on leaves and flowers. But she was not comparing like with like: she was comparing mainly early nineteenth-century West Country quilts with late nineteenth-century and twentieth-century Welsh and North Country ones. It seems possible that what she saw on the late eighteenth- and early nineteenth-century West Country quilts was the basic style common to much of Britain.

How did regional changes in style take place? As a traditional craft, quilting was part of an oral culture passed on from one generation to the next. In such circumstances, it is inevitable that the styles, patterns and techniques commonly used by one generation in a particular place will be passed on to the next. Not just a set of template outlines passed between the generations but a collective wisdom, gleaned from experience, of how to use particular patterns and how to achieve the necessary balance and precision of design. But each generation might alter the collective wisdom to a greater or lesser extent, contributing to a gradual evolution of style which, in geographically distant places, could move in different directions.

Once particular patterns became identified with a region, they were used with a regional consciousness and pride. So traditional quilting in Wales and the North of England became an expression of strength of attachment to the region and its culture. It was a way of saying 'this is part of me and where I belong' in the same way that traditional knitting patterns became specific to particular communities. Quilting became a means of expressing a regional identity, probably as important as any aesthetic intent on the part of the quiltmaker.

Regional styles and patterns did not, however, develop in complete isolation from other regions. Working people migrated from region to region, especially when their industrial skills or labour were required elsewhere. Miners from North-East England moved to South Wales, in the nineteenth century, when coal-mining families from the North-East took over some Welsh mines, and the occasional *feather* pattern on a Welsh quilt is perhaps evidence of this influence. Quilting patterns noted (but sadly not documented) in Langholm in the Scottish Borders were thought to have been influenced by the North Country tradition.[3] Men from the West of England moved north, as strike-breakers, in the 1870s to work in the Northumberland coal mines. One young lady from Devon, who moved with her family at this time, married and settled in Cramlington. Here she 'helped the Northumbrian women make quilts [for the Church] . . . there she learnt pattern quilting.'[4] So regional traditions could be either transferred or absorbed by the migrant elements of the population.

These population movements might explain the aberrant occurrence in one region of quilts which are clearly characteristic in style of another. Examples of this are the quilts in figs. 53 and 90. The quilt in fig. 53 was recorded and photographed in Dorset by Elizabeth Hake. Made in white cotton sateen with a frill on two sides, the whole style and particularly the use of the *bellows and star* pattern are typical of a standard North Country quilt of the late nineteenth/early twentieth century. Yet, on questioning the owner (Mrs Brown), it was discovered that the quilt was made by her aunt, in 1870, at Shroton in Dorset. Still suspecting a North Country connection, Mrs Hake wrote to Mrs Brown (1939) to ask if her aunt had ever been out of the county. Back came the reply:

. . . about my Aunt her parents and grandparents were Dorset people I never heard my Aunt say that they ever went very far out of Dorset my Aunt went to live in Shepton Mallett for a little while all the rest lived and died in Dorset . . .[5]

53. Wholecloth quilt in white cotton sateen (both sides) made at Shroton, Blandford, Dorset: 1870

Nevertheless, one cannot but suspect some outside influence. The quilt in fig. 90 was shown to me by a lady in Newcastle upon Tyne. Again, had I been given no information about where and when it was made I would have assumed it to be a North Country quilt. Yet the owner is certain that it was made by her great-grandmother, a blacksmith's wife in Fifeshire, around 1860.

Within living memory, traditional quilting has been an almost exclusively female craft, but this is certainly not true of recorded history. It is likely that many of the professional craft quilters of the period up to the mid-eighteenth century were men. Some we know of, like Walter Gale, of Sussex, who (around 1750) drew quilting designs on quilts, waistcoats and handkerchiefs.[6] One of the most famous of North Country quilters was a man – Joe Hedley of Northumberland (1750–1826). An itinerant tailor turned quilter, he was renowned for the quality of his quilts; and for the manner of his death – murdered by person or persons unknown! George Gardiner, the quilt designer from Allendale, had considerable influence on North Country quilt design in the late nineteenth century (pages 117–20).

More recently, frequent tales are told of the help given by menfolk in quilting families: though few did any stitching, they did sometimes help with the template-making and pattern-marking and threaded needles. One lady, brought up in Gateshead, remembers:

Father was very good at drawing and Mother would say what she would like for the new quilt. Father would draw it as she wanted and then he would take it to work and his friends in the pattern shop would cut them for him. The material used must have been thick cardboard because I don't think there was hardboard in those days [1920s] but it was firm and thick like that. Maybe it was something they used at the works. I can remember the designs, stars, half moons, crescent moons, diamonds, music notes and many more. One great highlight was as a surprise, Father brought home 'The Prince Of Wales' Feathers', it would be about 10 inches long and was placed at intervals all down the centre of a double quilt.[7]

But the attitude of menfolk in quilting families was not always so helpful. Some husbands, for a variety of reasons, deeply resented their wives quilting. When injury or illness forced a man to live off his wife's earnings, or when he was unable adequately to provide for his family, it was a considerable blow to his dignity and self-respect. Although circumstances might force him to tolerate a wife making quilts it was often deeply resented. The inescapable and intrusive presence of a large quilting frame in a small cottage, with perhaps only one main living-room, was another source of irritation. When one lady, the daughter of a quilt 'club' quilter was asked how her invalid father felt about her mother's quiltmaking, her instant reply was, 'He *hated* it.' Folk memory tells of another lady, the wife of a ship's captain from Sunderland, who made quilted petticoats in her spare time, in the late nineteenth century. Working secretly in an attic room overlooking the harbour, she would see her husband's ship return; so when he was approaching the shore, she abandoned her quilting and returned downstairs to her housewifely duties.

Of the women who made traditional quilts, some quilted for their own needs and some professionally. Mavis Fitzrandolph classified these quilters as: *home quilters* who quilted for themselves and their families; *village quilters* who quilted or marked designs to order; *itinerant quilters* who travelled around from house to house either making quilts or marking designs; and *quilt 'club' quilters* who made quilts for the subscribing members of a club. Home quilters and quilt 'club' quilters were often helped by members of the family and so the traditions and skills were passed between the generations. Daughters (and sons) might begin as children, threading needles – it was not an unusual chore for a child to be set on returning home from school. Once into her teens, or even earlier, a young girl might be put to the frame. Some only 'learned rough' from their mothers but later learned finer quilting from professional quilters. For some women, encouraging their daughters to help with quiltmaking was a way of keeping them at home. One County Durham lady 'started the youngest daughter at the frame to keep her at home' when all her older children had gone out to work.[8] It is a tale of dependency repeated elsewhere.

Itinerant quilters worked largely on their own but village quilters often took apprentices. In Wales a usual apprenticeship was a year but Mrs Peart of Allendale, Northumberland, was apprenticed to Elizabeth Sanderson for three years and worked as her assistant for four years after that, helping to mark the quilt designs for which Miss Sanderson was famous.

For the families who worked together around the frame, quiltmaking was an important communal activity. Many close family ties were cemented around both mat and quilt frames (fig. 54). In some parts of Britain, regular quilting parties or quilting days were also a feature of community life. But they never achieved quite the extensive community role of the American 'quilting bee' or the Ulster 'Quilting'. Laura Jones records that, in Ulster, Quiltings were a common social event up to the First World War and are remembered with

54. 'The Quilters' by Ralph Hedley, a North Country artist: 1883

great affection. 'The disappearance of the Quilting was one of the more regrettable changes in the pattern of rural social life.'[9]

In the North of England, quilting get-togethers were not unknown. In the nineteenth century, quilting feasts were held in parts of the West Riding of Yorkshire. 'When a woman had patched a bed quilt, she invited her neighbours and friends to help quilt it . . . tea and cakes were given; formerly a cold posset consisting of new milk, sugar, currants and rum (or beer).'[10] At the same time, in Weardale, community quilting parties were a regular feature with music and entertainment for the menfolk whilst the women quilted. A casual visit to a neighbour's might also provide opportunity for quilting. One Weardale man remembers:

To go prossing (chatting) to each other's houses was an almost regular thing . . . and while the menfolk talked and smoked and the bairns listened, the mother worked, mending, knitting . . . should a quilt be in the making (and what pieces of art they were, both in design and work, especially the patchwork ones) with two or three quilters helping them the talk would be a little harmless gossip on the ordinary doings of village life or, if some scandal got on the wing, their voices would sink to a whisper and heads draw a little closer lest the bairns should hear.[11]

With a touch of chauvinism and cynicism, a footnote to Thomas Wilson's poem *The Pitman's Pay* describes what he called a 'Quilting Day' (*c.*1850):

It was an awful sight to the male inmates of the house to see the quilting frame erected on the Monday morning, with many of the gossips in the vicinity set down to their highly-important labour. The whole attention of the mistress was given to these lady stitchers; nothing else was properly attended to as long as this important labour continued. The best creature comforts were provided for them, not omitting a drop of the bottle; for, as they gave their labour without fee or reward, the choicest fare was expected.[12]

Two types of quilt 'clubs' existed in the late nineteenth and twentieth centuries, particularly in North-East England. Both had an important economic and social role. In church quilting clubs, quilts produced by groups of women were sold at church fairs or 'bazaars' if they had not already been ordered. Though their chief aim was to raise funds, these clubs were often the one weekly opportunity for women to get together and exchange news, views and gossip. The quilt 'clubs' run by individual women were quite different (see page 122–5). Their purpose was family income and the club customer often belonged for philanthropic reasons. 'We did it to help out', one customer told me, which may help to explain why so many of these quilts have survived in almost perfect condition. Because they were not always needed, they were sometimes never used.

The quality of the quilts produced by the 'clubs' and groups was not always high. Many church groups in particular had no one with any design skill; their better quilts were often marked by the designers from Allendale and Weardale. Of the individual 'club' quilters, most achieved a high standard of workmanship. But the quality of design was not always so high, an almost inevitable result of the need to produce a quilt every two or three weeks.

One pressure which did help to maintain high standards of design and workmanship was competition. One lady recalls, 'if you were being married, well there was a great competition about getting a better design on our quilt than you had on yours.'[13] In many parts of the North-East of England, agricultural shows included competitive handicraft classes alongside their livestock ones. Competition amongst quiltmakers was intense, especially in Allendale and Weardale. One Allendale lady remembers that 'those [quilts] done for shows had to be done a very fine pattern, tiny little diamonds and the pattern had to be very close.'[14] For some, the money earned from show prizes was important extra income in the summer. One lady told me how her mother, who ran a quilt 'club' in Amble, would send her best quilt around the local shows. A first prize of 10s (50p) was often her reward – a not insubstantial addition to a weekly income of around £3 in the 1920s.[15]

The influence of the community in which quiltmakers lived and worked, the social and economic level that quilting occupied, and the regional consciousness engendered in the way the craft evolved were thus important influences. But just how extensive quilting was, even in the communities in which it thrived, is hard to quantify. Too little has survived and too little has been recorded for such an objective survey perhaps ever to be made.

7 English Quilts

NORTH COUNTRY

North Country quilting . . . is a craft which we Northerners looked upon as a very ordinary occupation and it is only the way it has been revived by the Women's Institutes and so admired by people in other parts of the country that we have come to realise the possibilities of our craft.
Jenny Hitchcock, Durham RIB quilter (*c.*1950)[1]

It is well known that quilting survived in the County of Durham well into the twentieth century – so well known that the term 'Durham Quilting' has come to be applied to the style more properly associated with all the northern counties of England where quilting was part of a way of life. Northumberland, geographically and culturally close to Durham, also had a particularly strong tradition, but quilting was part of rural life too in Yorkshire, Cumbria and the Isle of Man. Only Lancashire and Cheshire seem to have had no tradition, for here women were closely involved in textile manufacture, at first domestically and, later, in factories. Long hours working in the mill left little time for such a labour-intensive craft.

Quilts have been documented in the North of England as far back as anywhere in Britain. In a will of 1477,[2] 'unum twylt' is listed along with other bedding, and in the next century, isolated references (see Appendix) to 'a quilt', 'quilte' or 'twilt' also occur in the wills of gentry, merchants and wealthy widows. Quilts were not then common possessions; the will of Ralph Blaxton, a clerk of Blakiston, Durham, who died in 1569, gives what might be regarded as a typical list of bedding: 'It'm, I gyne to Robert Warke a fetherbedde, a bolster, two fustian blankets, a payre of shets, a happyng of whit and a lytyll on'see bedde . . .'[3] The use of the term *happyng* is worth further comment. It appears regularly, variously spelt, in wills from the sixteenth century onwards. But the word *hap* was used for a wool quilt in Northumberland, in living memory,[4] as was *twilt* for quilt. Was a *happyng*, then, some type of quilt? I think perhaps not. Taking, for analogy, contemporary lists of bedding from other parts of Britain, it seems more likely that a *happyng* was a wool bed rug of some kind and used, as a quilt would be, for the top covering of a bed. It was probably not until the second half of the eighteenth century that quilts began to displace *happyngs*, now generally called *happens*, as a common form of top bed cover.

Quilts were in use from the Middle Ages to the eighteenth century but chiefly by the noble and wealthy: in humbler homes, rough blankets and *happens* were the order of the day, as Celia Fiennes discovered when her journeys took her to Northumberland in the early eighteenth century:

This Hartwhistle [Haltwhistle] is a little town . . . here I was forced to take up my abode and the landlady brought me out her best sheets which served to secure my own sheetes from her dirty blanckets and indeed I had her fine sheete with hook seams to spread over the top of the clothes.[5]

Though the northern counties of England were geographically distant from London and the South-East, their thriving ports and towns were closely connected to the metropolis by sea trade. So fashionable trends of the capital were followed closely in the prosperous towns and cities of northern England. Evidence of this can be found both in archives and in the collections of local museums. The Castle Museum in York has a number of pieces of eighteenth-century wadded quilting as well as cord quilting – both fashionable forms of decoration of the period. The pieces include cot quilts, a christening set, a quilt-lined basket and pin-cushions, all in typical eighteenth-century style – in silk or satin fabrics, thin wool wadding and sewn with silk thread. But it is likely that some of these pieces, at least, were imported into the county, as were some bed quilts. Their role and common existence can be deduced from documents like the inventory of Nunwick House, Northumberland (fig. 52). Quilts by this time (late eighteenth century) were no longer only for 'best' rooms, but were to be found in every bedroom in this country house, though their style and quality (and age!) would vary from room to room.

The earliest surviving quilt known to have been made in the North of England is the unique and handsome Levens Hall quilt, pieced and quilted in 1708 (so it is said) by members of the family who then owned the hall near Kendal in Cumbria. The quilt is part of a set of mosaic-patchwork bed furnishings in Indian calicoes, quilted with an *allover* pattern of *square-diamonds*.[6] Despite the relative simplicity of its quilting, like most other quilts of this period it is associated with an affluent household.

Nineteenth century

Joe the Quilter   From the period around 1800 a number of quilts have survived of a quite different genre to the Levens Hall quilt. Quilts in cotton and homespun – patchwork and wholecloth ones – quilted in characteristic traditional style can be found in the collections of the museums of both the North of England and Scotland. Of these quilts, some are reputed to have been made by 'Joe the Quilter' who lived in the village of Warden, near Hexham in Northumberland. Joe the Quilter – or Joseph Hedley as he was properly called – has become a famous figure in North Country quilt history. But it was the manner of his death which ensured his legend; were it not for its violent end his life would have passed, as did those of other quilters, leaving little trace.

Joe the Quilter was born in 1750, and became a tailor by trade. At some point in his life he became a professional quilter, too, and if the quilts ascribed to him are any indication, he produced some finely worked and carefully designed quilts of a quality and beauty to rival any from other parts of Britain. The style of these quilts has, however, no individual or regional 'stamp'. The all-white 'best' quilt in the Bowes Museum, Barnard Castle, now showing signs of its age, contains intricate naturalistic patterns typical of early nineteenth-century quilts. So too does the orderly, but less closely worked homespun quilt (fig. 55) now in Carlisle Museum and Art Gallery. Joe Hedley also worked as an itinerant quilter and this homespun woollen quilt might well have been the type of quilt he made from home-produced cloth in the farms and cottages he visited.

In 1826, Joe Hedley was brutally murdered. He was 76. Though his life spanned a period of great social changes, these scarcely touched the quiet rural part of Northumberland that was his home. He quilted to the end of his days, but it clearly did not provide for his needs: he was on parish relief and neighbours kept a close eye on him to make sure he did not go short of food. But despite his poverty, Old Joe acquired a reputation as a man of some means: it seems he was killed for money he did not have. His murder caused a great stir in the region and its ripples went far beyond the immediate locality of Hexham (fig. 56). Despite

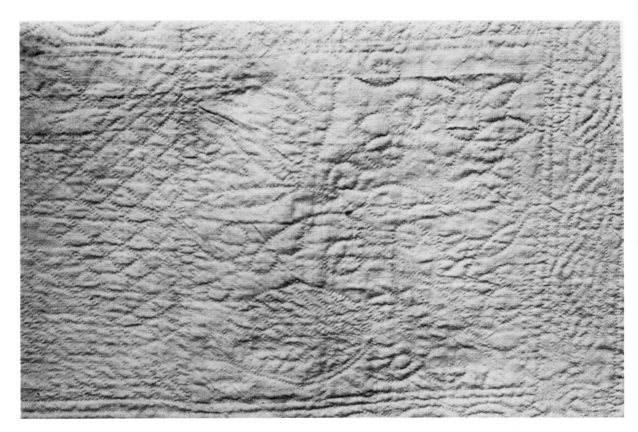

55. Detail of wholecloth quilt in yellow woollen homespun (reverse, light brown) quilted with a bordered design. Reputed to have been made by Joseph Hedley of Warden, Northumberland: early nineteenth century

widespread publicity, no murderer was ever found – hardly surprising at a time when many destitute people wandered the countryside – but some years later a vagrant in Carlisle confessed on his deathbed to the murder of old Joe.[7]

After his death, Joe's reputation as a quilter was, if anything, heightened. His quilts were treasured as much for their association as for their quality, and his place in local folklore was assured when a local poet, A. Wright, encapsulated his life in verse. It included the following lines:

> His quilts with country fame were crown'd
> So neatly stitched and all the ground
> Adorn'd with flowers, or figured round,
> Oh, clever Joe the Quilter![8]

The life and death of Joe Hedley represent the larger part of the few documented facts of quiltmaking in the first half of the nineteenth century in this part of England. But the evidence of surviving quilts shows just how widespread quiltmaking was. Patchwork quilts were especially popular, pieced in cotton prints but often backed with linen. Medallion quilts predominate (fig. 57), though mosaic and block designs were worked too. Appliqué quilts were also worked, but appliqué was used mainly in conjunction with patchwork on medallion quilts. Wholecloth quilts were either all-white 'best' quilts or of sturdy cloth, such as linsey-woolsey: the Manx Museum has eight wholecloth woollen quilts in which the predominant fabric is linsey-woolsey.[9] Carded wool was invariably used to fill these heavier wool quilts, for warmth rather than decoration was their purpose. But cotton wool was

A full true and particular Account of cruel and barbarous
MURDER,

Committed on the body of an Old Man, named Joseph Hedley, by cutting his Throat, and stabbing him in sixteen different places, near Hexham, on Tuesday last, Jan. 3, 1826.

THE unfortunate individual whose murder forms the subject of this paper, was an old man aged 76 years, and was the sole occupant of a lonely cottage, near Walwick Grange, four miles north of Hexham, in which he had lived from his infancy, and where, it would seem, he was doomed to meet with death in one of its most horrible forms. He followed the business of Quilting, and travelled round the country seeking employment in that occupation, and was well known to all, by the appellation of JOE THE QUILTER. It appears that by dint of industry in his calling, he had always been able to enjoy himself in an evening with company over a pint of ale, when it suited him, and honestly to pay for every thing he wanted with ready money : which gave rise to a rumour, that he had a quantity of money secreted about his cottage and person, and which no doub was the instigation of this cruel murder.

On Saturday morning as some people on their way to work, were passing by the cottage, they imagined they saw marks of blood on the snow, which lay on the ground about 6 inches deep and the appearance of a struggle having occurred there, which alarmed them for the safety of old Joe, with whom they were well acquainted.

They immediately proceeded to the cottage, but they found the door and window both fast as usual. They knocked and called some time but received no answer, which raised their suspicions still more, they then proceeded to the next house, for some instruments to break open the door, which they did, and found the walls of the cottage stained with blood in various places, and on a quilt in the frame was distinct marks of a bloody hand. And in one corner was found a towel on which the murderer, or murderers, had deliberately wiped the blood of his or their hands. They were now certain that some deed of horror had been committed, and on searching a kind of out house where he kept old wood and coals they discovered the desceased thrown upon the lumber, with his throat cut in three places, and sixteen stabs in his body, and both cheeks laid open with deep wounds evidently made with some instrument like a coal-rake.

It is supposed that the deceased had fought hard with the murderer, or murderers, and had escaped about one hundred yards from the cottage, where he had been overtaken, and evidently by the marks in the snow, a struggle had ensued, but the deceased had been overcome and dragged back, and murdered, after which the cottage door had been locked, on the outside, and the key taken away.

A Jury was summoned on Monday forenoon who sat on a view of the body and returned a verdict of "Wilful Murder against some person or persons unknown."

This circumstance is at present making a very great noise in the country where it happened, and as suspicion has not yet been decidedly thrown upon any one, every one looks at his neighbour with mistrust, and looks to see if any thing like murderer be wrote in his countenance, We hope it will not long remain so, and that the villian or villians, will not escape that punishment, which such an act of Atrocity so loudly calls for.

Printed by W. Stephenson, Quaker's Stairs, Gateshead.

57. Medallion quilt of cotton prints with backing of unbleached calico and quilted with an allover wave pattern. Made by Miss Dickinson, Kidburngill, Lamplugh, Cumberland: c.1850

widely used between cotton covers. Often the wadding was very thin. The patchwork quilts of Cumbria in particular were thinly wadded or even flat-quilted with no wadding at all: their purpose was to provide not warmth against winter chills but cheerful colour on top of the bed.

These early nineteenth-century quilts were quilted with both *bordered* and *allover* quilting designs. All-white 'best' quilts were worked in closely quilted *bordered* designs but many of the patchwork quilts were simply quilted in *allover* designs. Many – perhaps even the majority – of quilts from Cumbria and the Isle of Man were quilted with an *allover wave* pattern – an interesting link along this western side of Britain with the quilts made across the Irish Sea. On the eastern side of the Pennines *bordered* designs were usually worked even on patchwork quilts, though utilitarian quilts might have just a simple *allover* design.

The North Pennine Dales   It was probably in the first half of the nineteenth century that the seeds were sown which were to see quiltmaking assume such an important social role in the North Pennine Dales. Though geographically remote, the Dales of Teesdale, Weardale and Allendale were far from rural backwaters in the nineteenth century. Criss-crossed by mineral veins, they became important centres for mineral extraction, especially lead-mining. Prosperous, close-knit communities built up around these lead-mining centres; in 1861 Allendale Town reached its peak population of 6,400.

Within these communities, making quilts became an important part of domestic and community life. Intense rivalry developed amongst individual quilters, helping to maintain a standard of design and workmanship which lasted longer here than anywhere else in Britain. The collective expertise and confidence of quiltmakers in these Dales enabled them both to invent and to absorb new ideas, for here unique patterns and American influence emerged side by side, especially in the second half of the nineteenth century. Women were famed for the quality of their quilts. But quiltmaking was not just an individual domestic activity. A casual neighbourly visit might provide opportunity for social quilting (see page 110) and organized 'parties' were the occasion for song, dance and quilting too. A local historian records[10] Weardale parties where traditional fiddle-playing entertained the ladies working at the frame. After 1860, however, a drop in demand for lead began a rapid run-down of the mining industry, particularly in Allendale. By 1900 the population had halved, with many families moving to Tyneside and Wearside or to the coalfields of Northumberland and Durham. With them went their cultural traditions, including quiltmaking.

Quilt designers of Allendale and Weardale   For those who stayed in the Dales, quiltmaking remained an important part of domestic life into the twentieth century. Its position was strengthened when George Gardiner, who ran the local shop in the hamlet of Dorespool in Allendale, began a business sideline as a quilt designer in the second half of the nineteenth century. Already well known as a hat-trimmer, he turned his creative hand to drawing out quilting designs on wholecloth covers for others to quilt. How and why he turned to quilt designing is a puzzle: he is something of a mysterious figure known only from folk memory. But the profession he established in this remote corner of England is unique in quilt history and, moreover, continues to this day (though only just). Local tradition asserts it was his hand that developed the open, flowing style which influenced the North Country tradition of quiltmaking for the next hundred years.

George Gardiner trained others to design quilts in his characteristic style. He taught his two nieces and also took apprentice quilt designers, all of whom no doubt copied his highly individual style. In the 1870s he took another young apprentice, Elizabeth Sanderson. She was to become his most famous pupil and her influence on North Country quilting was, if anything, even greater than George Gardiner's.

Elizabeth Sanderson lived at Fawside Green, also in Allendale. After her apprenticeship with George Gardiner she worked as a quilt designer almost until her death in 1934, aged 73. For nearly 60 years she marked out designs on quilt tops sent by customers from all over the North of England and even further afield. She never married, but shared the family home with a sister, Mary, who took over most domestic responsibilities, leaving Elizabeth to work daily on designing quilts.

A niece remembers 'Aunty Lizzie' as 'quiet spoken, prim and proper, quick to work, but very exact',[11] and always with a pile of quilt tops waiting to be marked on the huge circular

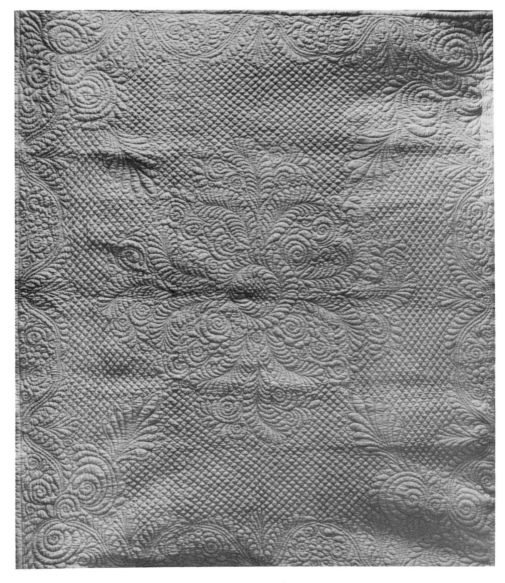

58. *Wholecloth quilt in cream cotton sateen (both sides) designed in Allendale and quilted by Mrs Rutherford when living in Rothbury, Northumberland: c.1915 (249 × 214 cm—98 × 84 in.)*

table which stood in the farmhouse parlour. She charged 1s 6d (7½p) for designing a quilt top – a price which seems not to have varied for as long as anyone can remember. She marked one, sometimes, two, a day, in blue pencil and with 'a lot of freehand' patterns, so even a conservative estimate must put the number of quilts she marked at several thousand.

Famed in the region for the quality of her designs and never short of work, Elizabeth Sanderson herself took apprentices. At any one time she might have up to four, from either Allendale or Weardale. Her first:

. . . was the daughter of a farming butcher at the head of Weardale. On leaving school at the age of fourteen, in the eighteen-nineties, she set out one morning to walk the six miles over the fell to Allenheads, carrying her provisions for the week – bread, butter, sugar and so forth. She served for one year without payment on either side going home at the end of each week and setting out again on Monday with her rations. She then became a paid hand, earning about four shillings a week and her board and lodging.[12]

59. Wholecloth quilt in cream cotton sateen (both sides) quilted with a bordered design in the style of George Gardiner: late nineteenth/early twentieth century

A later apprentice was Jennie Liddell of Allendale. She too began at 14, 'and served for a year without payment, taking her own food. She worked from eight in the morning until seven at night, with an hour off for dinner and half an hour for tea, and she served for six years, being paid two shillings weekly in the second year and finally four shillings.'[13]

The quilts marked by the designers of Allendale and Weardale in the 'Gardiner style' are easy to recognize and have survived in considerable number, often with the characteristic blue pencil markings clearly visible. With a few notable exceptions, the designers marked *bordered* designs on to wholecloth covers (figs. 58 and 59), particularly of cotton sateen, in a variety of colours; white, cream, blue, apple-green and pink were customers' favourites. The designs make extensive use of curvilinear patterns and freehand drawing, particularly scrolling to infill between patterns. Large centre motifs composed of a variety of pattern motifs and infills dominate the design and are rarely contained with lines of quilting, but usually 'flow' into the central field of *square-diamonds*. (One exception, however, is illustrated in fig. 93 where the centre motif is largely contained within two squares, one drawn square and the other on the diagonal to form an eight-pointed star.) Corner motifs are present, but can be of varying size and complexity. A single border pattern usually frames the design but occasionally a double border is used. Border patterns are seldom worked around a corner but a pattern such as a *rose* or *star* is set in the corner position. Those designers who worked from Weardale rather than Allendale did, apparently, use more feather patterns[14] – perhaps a conscious expression of their status as Durham (with which the *feather* is particularly associated) rather than Northumberland quilters. (Though geographically very close, Weardale is in County Durham whereas Allendale is in Northumberland.)

In looking at the many superb examples of 'stamped' quilts, of late nineteenth- and twentieth-century dates, a question arises. How far did Elizabeth Sanderson and her apprentices copy the style and patterns learnt from George Gardiner? Did they simply follow his lead or did they invent new patterns, new ideas and new embellishments? With no certain evidence of a George Gardiner quilt and the known biographical details of Elizabeth Sanderson, it does seem perhaps that she rather than he raised the design and quality of these 'stamped' quilts to a level that has never been equalled. Quilt designing was her life's work – the quilts she and her apprentices marked are carefully and confidently drawn but the precision is always full of vitality, never mechanical like the work of those who imitated but did not quite master her style. Her influence kept the style alive; once she died the quality of design gradually declined.

As well as wholecloth quilts, Elizabeth Sanderson and her apprentices also pieced patchwork covers, marked the designs on the covers, then sold them either direct to customers or via the packman – travelling salesman who sold goods from door to door. One favourite design was the *star* quilt shown in colour plate 10, and once an apprentice could confidently piece and mark a *star* quilt, she had learnt her trade. Another unique patchwork quilt pieced and designed by Elizabeth Sanderson is a red and white *basket* quilt in Beamish Museum (fig. 11).

When Elizabeth Sanderson died in 1934 her customers turned to a former apprentice, Jennie Liddell (Mrs Peart) of Allendale. Now married and with her own family, she carried on quiltmaking and designing until her own death at 83 in the 1970s. Up to the Second World War she was kept busy charging 1s 9d (8p) for an 'open' design and 2s 6d (12½p) for a closer one. It took her one to two hours to mark out a cover design. By 1967 her charges had increased to 9s (45p) and, by 1976, to 65p or 70p. Mrs Peart also took an apprentice who, though now an elderly lady, still designs the occasional quilt top, especially for the single surviving church club in Sunderland.

Around the turn of the century, and probably for much of the nineteenth century, it was the custom for a girl to have at least one quilt for her 'bottom drawer'. Many wedding quilts had their designs marked by the quilt designers for either the bride or her mother to quilt. I have even been told of 'club' quilters who made quilts professionally themselves, sending tops to Allendale for marking when a particularly 'special' quilt was required, for example, a daughter's wedding quilt: it seems these 'club' quilters recognized the limitations of their own design skills. 'Special' quilts such as these would be reserved for only occasional use – on a guest's bed, for the doctor's visit or when family and friends came 'to see the new bairn'. By the late nineteenth century, 'special' or 'best' quilts were almost always wholecloth ones: strippy quilts were considered second-best.

The role and influence of the quilt designers on the North Country quiltmaking tradition was very extensive. Though only a small number of designers ever practised the trade, everyone in the region who had any connection with quiltmaking knew of their existence and the quality of their designs. But they knew only by word of mouth, for until Mavis Fitzrandolph no one ever saw fit to record or comment in print on this unique trade.

The influence of the quilt designers had, however, two less positive effects. The development of their particular design style became something of a dead-end road and, with the passing of Elizabeth Sanderson, designs became stereotyped and mechanical. In addition, the facility offered by the designers at such low cost encouraged many to take the easy way and send all but strippy quilts to be marked by them. Thus, other quilters in the region never acquired the difficult and demanding skill of designing and marking out a quilt. In essence, the pool of design skills in the region was diminished.

The quilt designers of Allendale and Weardale were not the only professionals concerned with quiltmaking in the North of England. Itinerant quilters certainly existed in the nineteenth century, though there are fewer records of their existence in the North of England than in Wales. Mavis Fitzrandolph records: 'two sisters at Guisborough in Yorkshire, about 1870 to 1880, used to go to the big houses and farms for several weeks at a time, dressmaking and quilting being paid a few shillings weekly.'[15] Perhaps they made strippy quilts – popular in the Yorkshire Dales and usually quilted with simple open designs. I have also been told of itinerant quilters in the north of Northumberland, but not in any precise detail.

Of the quilters who worked from home, most were 'club' quilters. The quilt 'clubs' of North-East England began in the late nineteenth century and survived through to the 1930s (see page 122 for a full description of how these 'clubs' were established and operated). Other women, forced by circumstance to become bread-winners, combined quiltmaking with dressmaking, taking in washing and even midwifery (see page 98).

The church quilt clubs, which thrived in North-East England, seem to have begun in the mid-nineteenth century. Numerous churches and chapels were built in the growing towns and villages of Northumberland and Durham in the second half of the nineteenth century and strenuous efforts were made to raise funds for building. Selling quilts made by the quilt clubs and sewing groups was just one of many ways. They were sold at bazaars or direct to customers – never raffled, the fund-raising practice today. Raffles were a gamble – and since gambling was considered the work of the devil, it was hardly appropriate for a church group!

The quilts made in the second half of the nineteenth century show clear regional trends, both in style, fabric and usage. Both cotton and wool fabrics were used for quilt covers, but cotton wool or a blanket was the usual filling. Wool quilts, called *haps*, were made especially in Northumberland. It was the practice in sheep-farming districts to send wool to the local mills of Otterburn and Tosson (near Rothbury) to be spun and woven. Offcuts of this and the mills' own fabric offcuts were pieced into *haps*.

Cotton fabrics were, however, more commonly used than wool in the North of England. As piecing cotton scraps for patchwork quilts declined, cotton sateen was bought for both wholecloth and strippy quilts, though 'strippies' were also made with other cotton fabrics. Turkey red and white quilts were widely made as elsewhere in Britain, and American influence seems to emerge in the 'red, green and white' quilts. From 1860 sewing machines were increasingly used for making up the covers, for finishing edges and even for appliqué (fig. 60). Quilts were used both for 'best' and as everyday top bed covers. 'Best' quilts were usually closely worked wholecloth ones; strippy or patchwork quilts were for everyday use. Throughout the second half of the nineteenth century quilts were in common use in most 'ordinary' homes – the homes of agricultural and industrial workers in both town and country – especially in North-East England.

60. *Appliquéd quilt*
with red cotton
appliquéd motifs
machined on to white
cotton ground and
quilted with a strip
quilting design. Made
by Mrs Goldborough
of Pelton, Co.
Durham, as a wedding
gift for her daugher:
c.1884/5 (241 × 211
cm—95 × 83 in.)

Twentieth century

Despite the widespread use of quilts around the turn of the century – 'we all had quilts on our beds in those days' I was told[16] – quiltmaking itself was in decline in the North of England as a whole. In the North Pennine Dales and the mining districts of Northumberland and Durham, however, the tradition remained relatively strong up to the First World War for, in these areas, quiltmaking had developed a more important role in the social and economic fabric of the community. But in Cumbria, Yorkshire and the Isle of Man decline was more rapid.

'Club' quilters   One social tradition which did survive well into the twentieth century was the quilt 'club'. In the period up to the First World War, few mining villages and industrial areas of North-East England were without at least one quilt 'club'. Some continued through the 1920s and into the 1930s.

61. Wholecloth quilt
in cotton sateen quilted
with a bordered
design; made by Mrs
Shepherd, 'club'
quilter, Amble,
Northumberland:
1925–30 (254 × 214
cm—100 × 84 in.)

As rural families migrated to the pit villages of Northumberland and Durham, or to the terraced rows of industrial Tyneside and Wearside, they did not always prosper. Death or injury to the family's bread-winner was a disaster – sadly, a not infrequent one. Pit accidents in particular were common and left tragic consequences. When forced to become her family's bread-winner a woman who had learnt to quilt as a young girl often used her skill and established a quilt 'club'. A number of customers agreed to pay a weekly sum – 6d or 1s was usual – for a number of weeks until the full cost of the quilt was paid (usually around £3 10s). The weekly income financed material costs for each quilt (about £2 to £2 10s) and gave the quilter a small profit for her labour. (These figures relate particularly to the period 1920–30.) Her customers received their quilts in turn, often drawing lots to decide who received the first quilt, the second and so on.

Each quilt took an average of two to three weeks to make, though I have heard of some
who made a quilt a week. Both wholecloth and strippy quilts were made, of varying
quality. The design of many of these 'club' quilts became very standardized: in order to
work at the required rate, not too much time could be spent on elaborate design or close
quilting. So some of these quilts have a rather mechanical look, with large repeated motifs
poorly co-ordinated into simple *bordered* or *strip* designs. But others, despite the pressure of
circumstance under which they were made, have a quality and integrity of purpose which
transcends the rather restricted nature of their design (figs. 13 and 61).

The circumstances which forced one lady from Amble in Northumberland to start a quilt
'club', and the manner in which it operated have been graphically described by her
daughter:

my father was injured in the mines and he was denied compensation because the then doctors said his
injury was due to natural disease. But he never worked again after the accident, the roof of the pit fell
in on him and he was brought home battered and bruised from head to foot . . . he lay untreated for at
least a year . . . And so my mother stuck in to quilting to help us out with the housekeeping. I had to go
out and knock on peoples doors and ask them if they wanted to join our club. And some refused, but

many accepted until we had a sufficient number to start off and we would stop collecting customers when we had reached twenty. And then we would start off and it took my mother a fortnight to make a quilt, she would sit down to quilt at about 9 o'clock and carry on until dinner time without a break, then rest for an hour or two and start work about three o'clock and with a break only for tea, would carry on at least until 8 o'clock at night. And I helped with the housework and the quilt as soon as I was able to sit down.

Well my mother had many patterns, just at her finger-tips. She was able to draw them quite easily, but when she was tired of the pattern she would look around and she would copy anything that she would see, a curtain pattern, or a chair seat pattern, or anything that she would copy and put on a quilt . . . Well after taking a fortnight to make a quilt, my mother would have to bake on Sunday, it was the only time, then on Monday she would wash and she called that washing week, because she was always very tired and she would catch up on mending that week and extra housework . . . She always got the material for the quilts at the Co-op and when I collected for the club I took all that money for the club up to the Co-op every week and the manager just let us have what material we needed as we needed it . . . The customers chose their own colours. And this store, the Co-op manager, he gave us our own pattern book so that we always had it in the house so we could take it out to a customer and they would choose their pattern . . .

I collected the money every week, a shilling a week and took it straight up to the Co-op . . . A full sized quilt was three pounds ten . . . As far as I can remember the profit on a quilt would be a pound to thirty shillings. I always thought it would have been more profitable to scrub floors, but my mother wasn't built that way! She had to stay in anyway to be with my father who was injured in the pit.[17]

That these quilt 'clubs' flourished at a time when quiltmaking was dying in other parts of Britain, and quilts were regarded as old fashioned, is as much a comment on community attitudes as it is on the industry of the 'club' quilters themselves. If a small weekly contribution helped someone in difficult circumstances to maintain her dignity and feed her family, it was worth the effort. Despite the fact that good quilts were acquired for very modest cost, it is hard to escape the conclusion that the system survived, after the First World War, because of social rather than material need.

Patronage in the 1930s   When the Rural Industries Bureau (RIB) established its quilting scheme in the late 1920s and 1930s, Mavis Fitzrandolph did not have to look as hard in the North of England as she did in South Wales for good quilters to participate. Women's Institutes had already stimulated interest especially through Alice Armes, the national Handicrafts Organizer, a Durham lady herself. They were in touch with 'club' quilters in pit villages and able to recommend both the neediest and the best. A handful of women were chosen from County Durham (of whom all are now presumed deceased). Their workmanship was excellent (as was that of most 'club' quilters) but their design skills a little wanting. With encouragement to take more care in drawing patterns precisely and instructions on how to turn a corner, their standardized 'feather and roses' designs were improved, but they retained a stiffness and formality which set them apart from the fluid 'stamped' quilts being marked not too many miles away in Allendale and Weardale.

Like the Welsh quilters, these Durham RIB quilters were making wholecloth quilts for a luxury market. They were supplied with all materials by the RIB – silk and satin for top covers, sateen for backing and wool for filling – and paid for quilting by the square foot. A minimum of 1s 6d per square foot was paid initially, but this soon rose to 2s or 2s 6d depending on the closeness of quilting. For a very fine quilt, a quilter could therefore receive £10 to £12 – a vast improvement on pre-war rates.

As in Wales, the RIB scheme ceased with the outbreak of war in 1939. Its chief legacy in the North of England is the term 'Durham Quilting' which is too often erroneously applied to any quilt of North Country style.

The RIB was not, however, the only patronage scheme to bring employment into the depressed areas of County Durham. The role of the Northern Industries Workrooms' Clubs has recently come to light.[18] This organization, with Lady Cuthbert Headlam as its driving force, established two centres – one in Barnard Castle, the other in Langley Moor near Durham City. Luxury wholecloth quilts were made at both centres in satin and silk with lambs' wool, specially ordered from South Wales, for wadding. They were marketed in London for an average price of eight guineas but precisely how this marketing worked and whether it was linked in any way with the RIB scheme has yet to be discovered. Like the RIB in South Wales, this scheme used young girls as quilters rather than the older RIB quilters of Durham. Forty girls were employed in the centre at Barnard Castle, which opened in 1932. First, however, they had to be taught, for even in this Teesdale area, where only 20 years previously 'everyone around here had quilts', few young girls had learnt the craft. The quilters were paid 2s 6d a week to begin with, but by 1938 this had risen to £2. Despite this, local people thought the girls would be better employed in domestic service. Perhaps their attitude changed after a royal visit to the 1938 Exhibition, when quilts of peach and gold satin were presented to Princess Elizabeth (HM The Queen) and Princess Margaret. Little more than a year later, this scheme (like its RIB counterpart) ended when war intervened.

Post-war years   In the immediate post-war years, only a few women in the North of England continued to quilt. During the war years, materials were hard to obtain, though some, unwilling to let the habits (or hobbies) of a lifetime die, carried on quilting with what materials were to hand. The unusual and imaginative quilt in fig. 63 with its pieced *lovers' knot* was made by Mrs Armstrong of Northumberland during the Second World War. Some quilting classes even carried on through the war.

Of the women who had run quilt 'clubs' (which had virtually ceased even before the war), or had been involved in the RIB scheme, a handful took the occasional private commission. Some commissions came their way via the old London contacts; others were local orders. But in the North Pennine Dales of Weardale and Allendale the tradition of quiltmaking still survived, though to a lesser extent than in the early years of the century. The quilt designers continued to mark tops for so long as there was demand for their services, and those women for whom quilting was a particular source of pleasure and self-expression continued to make quilts for their families and even to order.

One such quilter was Mary Lough (fig. 64). Born in Weardale in 1886, Mary Lough absorbed the designs and technique of quiltmaking from an early age, threading needles for her mother by candlelight. But though she learnt quilting as a young girl, it was not until later years that most of her quilts were made. First she became a teacher then married and raised her family. Mary Lough was probably the first to take formal quilting classes under the auspices of a local education authority. Qualified to teach and with apparent artistic talent, she was well positioned to take advantage of the drive for adult education. Her classes began during the war years and she carried on teaching both in Weardale and further afield for many years. She died in 1968, aged 82.

Two of Mary Lough's pupils were to become very notable quilters in their own right. One was Florence Fletcher, herself a qualified teacher, who moved to Weardale when she married. Already a skilled needlewoman, whose grandmother had run a quilt 'club' in Ferryhill (Co. Durham), she was captivated by the quality of the quilts she saw in Weardale homes and resolved to become a quiltmaker herself. Florence Fletcher eventually became equally well known as a quiltmaker (fig. 65) and teacher and helped both Mavis

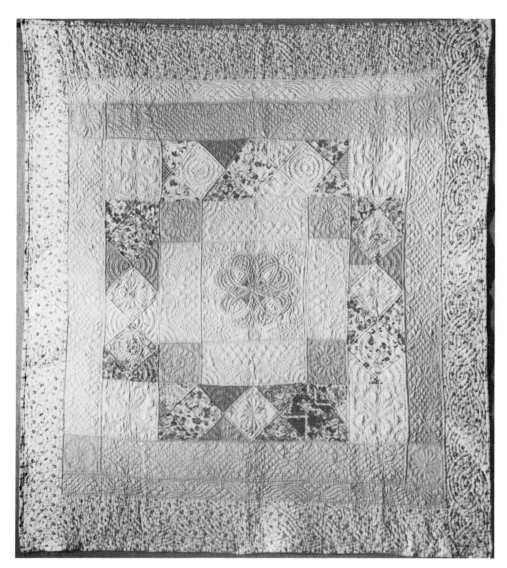

63. Patchwork and appliquéd medallion quilt with lovers' knot centre motif. Made with scrap cotton fabrics by Mrs Armstrong of Netherton, Northumberland, during the Second World War (213 × 189 cm—84 × 74 in.)

Fitzrandolph and Averil Colby in their research for their respective books. With Mavis Fitzrandolph she wrote the Dryad booklet *Quilting* – my early 'bible'.

Though already a quilter of quality and renown, Amy Emms (fig. 66) also attended Mary Lough's classes in the 1950s. Born in Sunderland in 1904, she learnt to quilt from her mother, who ran a quilt 'club' for many years. Mrs Emms always enjoyed quilting and, unlike her mother, was able to work for pleasure rather than need. Seeing the quality of her work at local exhibitions, the Local Education Authority encouraged her to teach but, not a qualified teacher, she needed a certificate. Hence the classes with Mrs Lough.

Over the last 30 years, Amy Emms has continued to teach quilting, first in the Sunderland area, then in Weardale to which she moved and, latterly, on Tyneside. She retired only in 1983 at the age of 80. She was and still is never without a quilt in the frame. The quality of her designs and superlative workmanship (fig. 67) have brought worldwide acclaim. In 1983 she was awarded an MBE in the New Year Honours List – an honour richly deserved

64. Mary Lough of Weardale

which brought almost as much pleasure to the new generation of quiltmakers who have come to know and respect her, as it did to Mrs Emms herself.

One further link with the tradition still survives in the North of England. In the church of Saint Mary the Virgin in Sunderland, the last surviving church club still meets regularly. Church quilting groups can be traced back as far as 1860 in the Sunderland area. For some reason, this was a particular stronghold of church groups, though they existed throughout Northumberland and Durham within living memory. Many were started in the early years of this century. 'Our Church . . . have made traditional quilts for as long as I can remember' one Sunderland lady recalled in 1978.[19]

The church groups provide an interesting parallel with the way quiltmaking has developed in Britain since the 'quilt revival'. In recent years many quilting groups have become established throughout Britain, with members coming together to make group quilts, just as the women in church clubs did. The main stimulus is not an economic one, like

65. *Wholecloth quilt in blue cotton poplin (reverse, pink) quilted with a* bordered *design by Mrs Florence Fletcher when living in Ireshopeburn, Weardale: 1958 (229 × 170 cm—90 × 67 in.)*

raising money for the church, but a social one of sharing a common interest in convivial company. But the quilts produced by these new groups are often used for charitable purposes, and raffled to raise money for a chosen charity. Their earlier North Country sisters would have approved the end – but not the means!

66. *Amy Emms MBE*

Characteristics of North Country quilts

Many nineteenth- and twentieth-century quilts from the North of England have survived in both public and private hands though, sadly, few have any information about their makers with them. Nevertheless, it is possible to identify from these quilts the distinctive directions in which quiltmaking evolved in parts of the region. Certain patterns and the way in which they were used became standard at some point in the nineteenth century and were followed, with varying degrees of success, by quiltmakers through to the present day. It should be emphasized, however, that although it is possible to identify 'regional' patterns,

67. *Wholecloth quilt in ivory polyester satin made by Amy Emms: 1977 (233 × 215 cm—92 × 84 in.)*

the use of a particular pattern is no guarantee that the quilt was made in the region with which the pattern is usually associated. Ideas did travel. The overall design and use of fabrics are as much a guide to the origin of a quilt as the patterns themselves. Even taking all these factors into account, there can be no certain identification, only a probable one.

Allover designs and filling patterns   On quilts made in the nineteenth century, North Country quilters used all the simple filling patterns – *square-diamonds*, *shell*, *wave* and *wineglass*. *Wave* quilting is particularly common on quilts made in Cumbria. On twentieth-century quilts, *wave* and *shell* fillings are less common; *square-diamonds* and *wineglass* are the popular filling patterns on these quilts.

These simple filling patterns were used both as infill patterns and as *allover* designs but more complex *allover* designs include *bellows and star*, a widely used North Country pattern.

Bordered designs   On North Country quilts made up to *c*.1850, *bordered* designs show many similarities to those produced elsewhere in Britain. Elaborate naturalistic designs were worked with two or three borders delineated by lines of quilting and, not infrequently, geometrically divided. But, even in this early nineteenth-century period, there was an evident tendency to free-flowing leaf and flower patterns – the beginnings of the style which later became identified with the region.

In the second half of the nineteenth century, *bordered* designs developed along two lines. The first line was that identified with the quilt designers of Allendale and Weardale and described on pages 119–20. The flowing nature of these designs was reinforced by the lack of containing lines delineating the elements of the pattern, i.e. lines of quilting separating the centre and corner motifs, and borders, are usually absent from these designs. The second simpler line was followed particularly by 'club' quilters who produced simplified versions of *bordered* designs which could be quickly worked. Taking the basic format of centre motif, corner motif and border, they quilted more open designs with relatively simple motifs, often rather stiffly organized. Inevitably there was a degree of interweaving of the two lines as the better home quilters strove to improve the quality of their own design by copying the style of the quilt designers.

Of the motif patterns used by North Country quilters, *roses* and *feathers* predominate. They appear in a variety of forms and sizes; *feathers*, in particular, were associated with Durham quilters. But other common motif patterns include *scissors*, *lovers' knot*, *fan* and leaf and flower patterns of wide variety, including *tulip*, *sunflower*, *privet leaf*, *cowslip leaf* and *honeysuckle leaf*.

Border patterns used on *bordered* designs include the *running feather*, *hammock* and its variations like *cord and tassel*, *Weardale chain*, *bell*, *plait* and the variations of the *cable twist* pattern including (from the 1930s onwards) the *feather twist*. *Worm* or *trail* patterns (wavy-line patterns of some antiquity) were also popular, again in a variety of forms.

Strip designs   *Strip* designs were quilted not only on to strippy quilts, but on to wholecloth and patchwork quilts too. They varied enormously in quality from crudely worked simple designs to precise and closely quilted intricate ones. All the popular border patterns used on *bordered* designs were also commonly used on *strip* designs but, in addition, repeated motifs like the *rose* or *feather-wreath* were worked down the length of a quilt.

A North Country quilt can also be identified from its general style and use of fabrics. Wool was rarely used for wadding after 1850; instead, cotton wool or an old blanket were the usual fillings. The edges of North Country quilts were sometimes machine-stitched, usually with a double row of stitching, after about 1860; indeed, this became the commonest method of finishing on late nineteenth- and twentieth-century quilts. As for colour, in contrast to the bold colour combinations of the Welsh, North Country quilters had a quieter taste, preferring either white or pastel shades or combinations of the two for their wholecloth and strippy quilts. Even the later nineteenth-century patchwork quilts had a distinctly pastel look to them. In the 1920s and 1930s – and later in the 1950s – a taste for silk and satin quilts developed, though these were still in relatively light tones.

Because of this colour choice, the style of design and the often thin filling, many North Country quilts, especially the late nineteenth-century ones, have a gentle quality, a quiet tranquillity, which belies the often harsh, demanding environment in which they were made.

WEST COUNTRY

If a girl has not made a quilt before she is twenty-one no man will want to marry her
Old Devon saying[20]

Were it not for the extensive fieldwork and research done by Elizabeth Hake in the 1930s, little would be known of a quilting tradition in the counties of the West of England. Following the chance discovery of a Devon quilt in 1933, she began a search to discover how extensive traditional quilting had been in this corner of England. She uncovered many old quilts from the counties of Cornwall, Devon, Somerset, Dorset, Wiltshire and Hereford and established contact with a number of older women who remembered quilts and quilted petticoats being made. They were able to describe in some detail the patterns and techniques used. Elizabeth Hake published the results of her work in 1937, but continued her research until war intervened in 1939.

Fifty years on, I am able to add little to her account of the West Country tradition. It is a sad fact that, of over 30 West Country quilts she recorded and photographed, only one is known to survive. Some county museums, notably Somerset and Hereford, do have small collections of local quilts but as elsewhere, the more prestigious institutions have concentrated on collecting bourgeois forms of needlework and have largely ignored traditional quilts. From living memory, in this part of England, quilting has disappeared: the suggestion that there was a local tradition now meets with some surprise and even disbelief.

From surviving quilts in local museums and the archive compiled by Elizabeth Hake, it is clear that wadded quilting (known in the West Country as 'hard' quilting) was a traditional home craft in this part of Britain, as in many other rural areas. It was used for both quilts and quilted petticoats from at least the middle of the eighteenth century through to the late nineteenth century. But the decline of the craft in the years preceding the close of the nineteenth century was rapid and, by 1900, it had all but died.

Though the eighteenth-century green silk quilt in fig. 68 probably came from a wealthy household, other known West Country quilts are almost all traditional 'cottage-style' ones. A few were wholecloth quilts of homespun or cotton fabrics, wadded with wool, and a single example of a strip patchwork quilt survives in Somerset County Museum in Taunton. Other recorded patchwork quilts include mosaic and block designs pieced in a restricted number of probably bought fabrics (fig. 70). But most were scrap patchworks pieced in medallion designs of varying pattern and complexity (fig. 71). One Cornish lady recalled her mother making quilts in the 1860–70 period: 'One side of the quilt was always patched. She was a careful woman and every scrap of cotton print was used up for patchwork.'[21] Up to 1850, these medallion quilts were often backed with linen and it is on the reverse side that the quilted design can be most clearly seen.

Inevitably, the designs quilted on to these West Country quilts varied with the nature of the covers and the use of the quilt. Simple *allover* designs were worked on utility quilts: an unusual one of large concentric circles was noted on the strip patchwork quilt in Taunton. Using an *allover* pattern of *square-diamonds* must have been widespread, for the Devon and Cornish women who came north to Northumberland in the 1870s with their strike-breaking husbands had never seen 'pattern quilting' but only 'plain diamonds'. Another utility quilt – a linsey-woolsey one of unknown date but probably West Country origin – is quilted with a geometric but simple *bordered* design (figs. 72 and 73). Though worn and badly marked, this unique quilt is a rare example of a quilt type which may have been

68. Wholecloth quilt in green silk quilted with a bordered quilting design, probably West Country: eighteenth century

widespread in the eighteenth and early nineteenth centuries. Its coarse linsey-woolsey covers, perhaps homespun and home-dyed, are wadded with wool and coarsely though evenly stitched to produce a quilt for warmth rather than decoration. Its present condition indicates all too clearly why such quilts were discarded and destroyed once they had reached the end of any useful life.

All-white wholecloth quilts ('best' quilts) and some medallion quilts (perhaps also 'best' quilts) were quilted with *bordered* designs of beauty and intricacy to match any from elsewhere in Britain. Sadly, surviving photographs of these quilts are too poor now for reproduction and it is only possible to reproduce some of their detail (figs. 74 and 75) but

69. Border detail of quilt in fig. 68.

70. Patchwork and appliquéd block quilt in red, green and white cottons quilted to co-ordinate with the cover design. Made in Devon: nineteenth century

many were illustrated in Elizabeth Hake's own book.

West Country quilters considered their designs to be 'naturalistic'. Elizabeth Hake records:

According to the aged quilters . . . floral designs in the West were made from nature. One of them recalls the fact that her mother and grandmother used to pick sprays of oak leaves, ivy, clover, and even thistles, bringing them home to study in the evenings before making the great decision as to which should form the basis of the design for a new quilt.[22]

Comparing these West Country *bordered* designs to similar quilts from other parts of Britain, it is not easy to be sure if this 'naturalistic' style was a regional one or simply a reflection of a common quilt style throughout Britain. I am inclined to the latter view, though so few quilts, of the early nineteenth century particularly, have survived from other regions that comparisons are not easy. But those that have survived do show a use of similar naturalistic patterns: using baskets or vases of flowers as centre or corner motifs was a notable common practice up to 1850. Perhaps this 'naturalistic' style was a common one throughout Britain which followed from the style of wadded quilting used on eighteenth-century quilts

72. *Wholecloth quilt in linsey-woolsey quilted with a* bordered *design, probably West Country: c.1800*

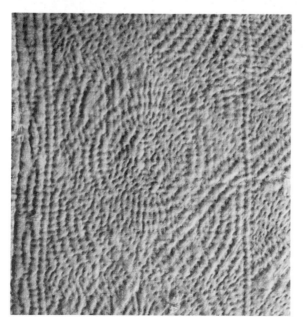

73. *Border detail of quilt in fig. 72*

74. Centre detail from wholecloth side of medallion quilt made by Mrs Louisa Cook, Yarcombe, Devon: c.1820–40

and petticoats. It was then used, with little regional change, through to the mid-nineteenth century. The West Country quilters, in their choice of pattern, may well have emphasized this 'naturalistic' style but they did not seem to develop it in any noticeable direction.

There are apparent links, however, in the patterns and styles of West Country and Welsh quilts. Both show frequent use of *spiral* motifs and geometric border patterns: *church windows*, the pattern of overlapping half circles, is often regarded as a characteristic Welsh pattern but it occurs on West Country quilts too. And the pattern used on the outer border of the Welsh quilt in fig. 77 is seen in similar form on West Country quilts. Such a link is not altogether surprising: there were close trading connections between South Wales and the West Country across the Bristol Channel.

75. *Border and corner detail of wholecloth quilt made by Mrs Jane Magan, Bridgewater, Somerset: 1807*

West Country quilts were made both by home quilters, for their own use, and by professional quilters. Quilting was commonplace up to about 1880, using techniques little different from elsewhere. One Devon family of sisters 'remember that if ever one of them chanced to be idle she was bidden by her mother to "get on with the quilt", which, set up in its frame formed a normal part of the furniture in most living rooms.'[23] Most home quilting, in fact, seems to have been done by young girls:

Judging by family stories and memories it seems that in a great many cases quilts were made by girls between the ages of fifteen and twenty-five, before they married. A girl would begin by being taught by her mother to make what was needed for the family's use, or to repair an old quilt, and by the time she was really proficient she would embark on quilting for her future home. After her marriage, almost inevitably it appears that no further work of the kind could be undertaken by a young wife until her daughters grew old enough to learn from her in turn.[24]

Though there is no record of itinerant quilters in the West of England, village quilters who quilted to order were certainly known. Elizabeth Hake records 'professional quilting ... in some parts of Cornwall, where as much as 10s, 15s or £1 would sometimes be paid for an elaborately worked quilt.'[25] She does not, however, record whether this was just the cost of quilting a pieced top or whether it represented the total cost of a new quilt. Other women did just quilt ready-pieced tops: 'one [woman] who lived in North Devon can remember that her mother and her mother's friend made the patchwork sides for their quilts, and passed them on to a neighbour to quilt, for which she charged 3s 6d each.'[26] Perhaps at that price, they only got 'plain-diamonds'! Miss Stamp, the postmistress (yes really!) from Luppitt, Devon, from whom Elizabeth Hake acquired much of her information, was told 'by an old lady over 80 [that] she went to a school of quilting when young near Exeter'.[27] Following this information back would suggest the school was in existence around 1865. Miss Stamp also remembered 'seeing the black skirts in the frames and they were sent to London',[28] a suggestion that black quilted petticoats were fashionable items in the 1860s and not just worn by country women.

By the end of the nineteenth century, many West Country quilts had suffered the fate of those elsewhere. Now regarded as old-fashioned, they were either 'worn out on the beds of grandchildren' or 'used in their last stages under mattresses'.[29] A sad fate for such beautiful pieces of work. And were it not for the energy and enthusiasm of one lady the fact that they had existed at all would not be known.

REST OF ENGLAND

When quilting was largely in professional hands – up to around the mid-eighteenth century – London was probably the chief centre of the trade. A 1709 copy of the *London Gazette* records one 'Michael Scott of Fetter-Lane . . . Quiltmaker'.[30] But when quilting became a traditional craft in rural Britain, it seems not to have become established to any degree in South East England, East Anglia, the Midlands and the Home Counties. Certainly no tradition survived into the twentieth century. Whether any quilting tradition did exist, for which material and documentary evidence have not so far been discovered, is an open question.

Two factors may, in part, explain the apparent absence of a quilting tradition in these regions of England. Traditional quilting was done, for the most part, by women in their own homes. In the Midlands, East Anglia and parts of the Home Counties there has been a long tradition of female employment in home, farm and factory, so women's lives were centred less on domestic responsibilities than in some other parts of Britain. This left little time for a labour-intensive craft like quilting. And, being closer to the metropolis, these regions were more influenced by bourgeois taste and attitudes than remoter areas. Though patchwork was a popular craft throughout the nineteenth century, quilting may perhaps have been regarded as too proletarian.

Nevertheless, it is surprising that little has so far emerged from some of the more rural counties where social and economic conditions had much in common with the parts of Britain where traditional quilting was firmly established.

8 Welsh Quilts

I have the make of the frame and my mother sitting there hour after hour, very vivid in my mind.
George Davies, son of a Pembrokeshire quilter.[1]

Quilts have been recorded in Wales as far back as the sixteenth century. The earliest known reference is in the will of the last feudal baron of Powys Castle (1551) which records three quilts, one of red satin, one of taffeta of 'changeable colour' and a third unspecified quilt in the nursery. The sixteenth, seventeenth and eighteenth centuries provide further scattered references (see Appendix, page 158) to show that quilts and quilted items were in common use in Wales throughout these centuries. But their association is not, in the main, with small one- or two-roomed cottages but with larger homes – a reflection of their general use by more affluent and aristocratic sections of society.

Two Welsh quilts in the collection of the Welsh Folk Museum at St Fagans are among the oldest known surviving examples. Both have come from country houses – one in North and one in South Wales – and date from the eighteenth century. The quilt from Plas Llanfair, Caernarvonshire (Gwynedd) is an embroidered one quilted in an *allover* pattern of *diamonds* – a type and style which could be found in any country house in Britain in the eighteenth century. The quilt from Tredegar Park, Monmouthshire (Gwent), however, is a typical, eighteenth-century wadded quilt, filled with wool. The top cover is of yellow silk, pieced of numerous fragments in much the same manner as the silk quilt of similar age in fig. 68: it seems likely both quilts were made from re-used fabrics.

The Tredegar Park quilt[2] (fig. 76) is quilted with a *bordered* quilting design containing all the characteristic hallmarks of this traditional form: a circular centre motif set in a *diamond-filled* centre field with quarter circles repeating the centre motif at the corners of the centre field. Unusually, half circles also repeating the centre motif are set centrally along the sides of the centre field, which is surrounded by three borders of increasing depth, each separated from the next by a double row of quilting lines. Each border is filled with a different pattern, the first of infilled circles and the second of crude semi-circles. The final border is geometrically divided into triangles with the outer triangles filled with *wave* infill. The inner triangles have a symmetrical filling pattern of leaves and scrolls of a style which later became common on quilts made both in Wales (fig. 77) and the West of England. Though of the same type and age as the quilt in fig. 68 the style is simpler, less florid, and, interestingly, has much in common with the later nineteenth-century quilts recorded from the West of England.

Nineteenth century

In nineteenth-century Wales, quilting was widespread and popular, especially in the old rural counties of Pembrokeshire and Carmarthenshire (now Dyfed). In many of the farmhouses and cottages women quilted for themselves or for a living: even in country houses quilts were still made, though mainly 'downstairs'. 'Quilts were part of our lives, like table and chairs', said one Welsh quilter.[3] All types of quilts were made – wholecloth, patchwork, appliqué and even strippy quilts – though the latter were much less common than in the North of England and most often utilitarian. Patchwork, though bold and colourful, was often of a more utilitarian nature, with medallion quilts by far the most popular (figs 77 and 78). Some of these scrap patchworks were carefully and intricately quilted, though in *bordered* designs which ignored the patchwork design. Fig. 16 shows the wholecloth side of a patchwork quilt made in Pembrokeshire around 1840. This carefully planned and skilfully worked *bordered* design is the work of a true craftsperson but the interest lies not just in its quality but in its style. Despite the *cable twist* outer border (typical of North Country quilts in the twentieth century), it contains elements which can be thought of as characteristically Welsh, namely the curved and bent veined leaves. The spirals found on both Welsh and West Country quilts of this period are also much in evidence both in formal motif patterns and as infills.

Appliquéd quilts were less common, but an example is the quilt in fig. 79, made in

76. Wholecloth quilt in yellow silk quilted with a bordered design, Tredegar Park, Monmouthshire: mid-eighteenth century

Pembrokeshire and inscribed *Mary Lloyd 1840*. The appliquéd wreath and bows suggest this was a marriage quilt and probably the finest in the customary set of six quilts which formed part of a Welsh girl's dowry. The use of a *running spiral* pattern for the outer border is a feature of some Welsh and West Country quilts of this period but later it became one of the distinguishing features of only Welsh quilts.

Welsh quilts were usually wool-filled but both cotton and wool fabrics were used for the covers. Medallion quilts of cotton prints – little different from those made in other parts of Britain – were produced for both 'best' and 'everyday' quilts. As elsewhere, cotton sateen was widely used in the second half of the nineteenth century, but the Welsh were particularly fond of using wool fabrics, like flannel and tweed, both for patchwork and wholecloth quilts. 'One Carmarthenshire quilter, born in 1870, recalled that cloth woven in the local mills of wool sent in by neighbouring farmers was popular for quilts in her youth, in two colours, such as rose or blue with maroon.'[4] The heavier weight of the wool fabrics made coarser stitching inevitable, but the deeper depressions of the stitches created a more strongly sculptured look to the quilted design.

The Welsh had a fondness for strong colours – red, magenta, maroon, dark blue, green, purple, brown and even black – in contrast to the prettier pastel shades North Country quilters preferred. Red and white quilts were as popular in Wales as elsewhere and, towards the end of the century, printed cotton sateen in paisley and floral prints and 'in the grandest of colours' became fashionable for quilts and for general furnishing use. This was, however, something of a retrograde step, for the printed fabrics detracted from the quality of the quilted design and led to a decline in standards. Mavis Fitzrandolph believed it was this use of

77. Medallion quilt quilted with a bordered design; Welsh: early nineteenth century

78. Medallion quilt quilted with a bordered *quilting design, made by Esther David (1821–98) of Llanfabon, Glamorgan (210 × 206 cm)—83 × 81 in.)*

79. Medallion quilt in multicoloured cotton with appliquéd centre and quilted with a bordered *design.* Inscribed *Mary Lloyd 1840: from Cardiganshire (Dyfed) (254 × 254 cm—100 × 100 in.)*

strongly patterned materials, together with the low rates of payment, which brought the technique of quilting to such a low state in South Wales.[5]

The designs quilted on to these nineteenth-century Welsh quilts reflected their status. 'Everyday' quilts were quilted either with an *allover* design or a simple *bordered* one (fig. 80); rarely, a *strip* quilting design might be used. These utility quilts were coarsely stitched with linen or cotton thread and often filled with either an old blanket or a variety of scrap materials. They were thick and heavy, but no doubt very warm; unlike most North Country quilts they were used in place of blankets. One Welsh lady remembers[6] picking open the quilt on her childhood bed to see just what was inside. Her reward was a glimpse of the pieces of shirt flannel, old sheets, net curtains and other scrap fabrics often thickly layered into these 'everyday' quilts. By contrast, 'best' quilts were wool-filled and carefully quilted with elaborate *bordered* designs.

Many women in Wales were home quilters working for their own or their families' needs. It was a matter of pride with some mothers to make at least one quilt for each son and daughter before they were married. But many a Welsh bride had six in her dowry; some she might have made herself from the time she first learnt to sew. Home quilters often quilted together; as well as families, neighbours would work together, making a quilt for each in turn.

Professional quilters were commonplace in South Wales in the nineteenth century. Village quilters made quilts to order, with the customer supplying materials, but it was poorly paid work with an average price of only 4s 6d (23p) to 5s (25p) for making a quilt. Single women who needed to provide for themselves or dependent relatives often became village quilters. Some combined quilting with other skills such as dressmaking. During her extensive field work in Wales, Mavis Fitzrandolph recorded in some detail the working lifestyles of professional quilters. She later wrote:

One quilt a fortnight was said by several people to be the usual rate of output for a professional quilter, working alone, but there were many variations. As in the north some worked late 'with a candle on the quilt' and others only by daylight. Mrs Katherine Evans, fifty years ago [c.1900] worked only eight days on a handsome quilt with a good deal of close stitching in it, which she was still [in 1950] keeping

80. Wholecloth side of patchwork quilt quilted with a bordered design, made in Carmarthenshire (Dyfed): c.1860 (248 × 208 cm—98 × 82 in.)

81. Quilters at Solva, Pembrokeshire (Dyfed): 1928

unused for her niece. Mrs Eleanor Williams said it took her two weeks to make a quilt, working from eight or nine in the morning till about six and only stopping to eat (but her working time must have been shorter in winter, for she only worked by daylight); what I have seen of her work is much rougher than Mrs Evans's, with simple patterns. Mrs Colman, an elderly woman quilting for her living, completes a quilt in four or five days and it is well drawn and sewn though the patterns are big and widely spaced with no close work.[7]

One of the most famous village quilters was Mary Jones of Panteg, Cardiganshire (now Dyfed), commonly known as 'Mari Panteg'. Her fine quilts were treasured by her customers; she was never short of orders. She worked at her quilts 'morning and night' sewing as well with her left hand as she did with her right. She often worked with an apprentice who neither received nor made any payment during the period of apprenticeship, but was expected to help with jobs around the house as well as with quiltmaking.

Itinerant quilters were regular visitors to the farms of South Wales and parts of Mid-Wales. The farmer's wife provided materials, but the quilter brought her own frame and settled into the household for so long as it took to produce the number of quilts required. This might be up to a couple of months if the quilts for a dowry were to be completed. Sometimes itinerant quilters worked in groups – perhaps two or three – quilting at the frame together. 'One gets the impression', records Mavis Fitzrandolph, 'in talking to the old ladies who were itinerant quilters in their younger days, that their life was a pleasant and interesting one.'[8] They were also slightly better paid than the village quilters, taking into account that food and board was free; 9d (4p) to 1s (5p) a day was the average up to 1900.

Quilts and quiltmaking were very much a part of everyday life in South Wales throughout the nineteenth century. The traditions and skills associated with the craft became firmly embedded in rural lifestyles, but how far north this extended is difficult to ascertain. Certainly quilts were made in parts of Mid-Wales and it is difficult to believe the tradition did not extend into North Wales too. Cottage-style unquilted patchworks have been recorded in North Wales and in recent years evidence suggests, but cannot confirm, that quilts were made here too.

By the close of the nineteenth century, quiltmaking still flourished in many rural areas, but it had past its peak. As families migrated to industrial towns and mining valleys the custom they had provided for professional quilters went too. Some took their skills with them and continued to make quilts for themselves, for customers and even for shops – especially if hard times prevailed. But the change which had already affected much of Britain – the fashion for new machine-made bed covers – was beginning to be felt in Wales too.

Twentieth century

The twentieth century had scarcely begun when the first attempts to promote traditional Welsh quilting were made. In recognition of the high level of craftsmanship involved in this traditional work and the danger it faced from machine-made competition, quilts were included in the exhibitions of Welsh industries of 1903 and 1904, held in London. The quilting seems to have excited little general interest, providing only a degree of satisfaction to those who won certificates for their work.

Up to the 1930s quiltmaking was still practised in South Wales (figs 81 and 82) but never to the same extent as in the previous century. Some fine wholecloth quilts were produced but 'everyday' quilts were now covered in figured sateen or paisley prints – fabrics popular in the first decade of the century. In the early 1920s quilting declined rapidly despite the

82. *Quilters at Solva,*
Pembrokeshire
(Dyfed): 1928

83. *The Porth quilting*
group: 1938

efforts of the Welsh Industries Association to arouse public interest. A handful of itinerant quilters and professional quilters still worked and 'club' quilters were recorded in the mining valleys by Mavis Fitzrandolph. But precisely when, where and how they worked is not known, in contrast to the wealth of detailed information on the 'club' quilters of North-East England.

The Rural Industries Bureau Scheme   In 1928, the Rural Industries Bureau (RIB) sent Mavis Fitzrandolph to Wales as well as to Durham in its quest to revive quilting in these areas. She met some resistance from municipal organizations who declared that 'quilting was a dead or dying industry in Wales, that no work of any value would be found and that, if it were, no one beyond the Principality would want to buy it.'[9] Despite these doubts, she did manage to track down a number of quilters and the Bureau financed initial orders for the most promising. The first exhibition of their work was held in Muriel Rose's Little Gallery in London in 1928. It was a great success and brought a flood of orders.

It soon became obvious that, though fine traditional skills still survived in rural South Wales, there were not enough women in the mining valleys who could work to the very high standard needed for the London market. Mining districts were the areas the Bureau most wanted to help for it was here that the effects of the Depression were hardest felt. So classes were organized to teach both experienced quilters and new workers, especially young girls. Six classes were opened; Porth in the Rhondda (fig. 83), Aberdare, Blaina, Merthyr Tydfil, Abertridwr and Splott (Cardiff). All were taught by experienced Welsh quilters and the importance of maintaining the native tradition was insisted upon. One of the best-known teachers was Jessie Edwards of Porth (fig. 84); renowned for the quality of

84. Miss Jessie Edwards, quilting teacher at Merthyr Tydfil and Rhondda, 1930–59

85. Cot-sized quilt produced in Wales under the RIB scheme

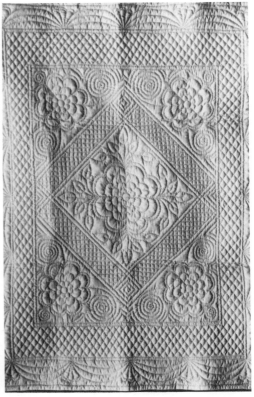

her work, she made an outstanding contribution to the scheme and continued to teach at local education authority classes until 1959.

Under the guiding hands of their teachers, Welsh RIB quilters soon produced work of a high quality (figs. 85 and 86), inventing new patterns and adapting traditional ones to new uses, for example on cushions and dressing gowns. Payment was better than it ever had been for traditional quilting; there was either a set scale of charges for particular items or they were paid by the square foot. The quilts made were invariably wholecloth ones in silk, sateen or poplin – poplin was especially popular in Wales.

The RIB scheme continued right through the 1930s. Major boosts both to the scheme and

86. Wholecloth quilt quilted with an innovative bordered design. Made under the RIB scheme by a young Welsh quilter, Miss G. K. Evans: c.1930–5

to the confidence of the quilters came from exhibitions arranged in London. One in particular, at the Dorchester Hotel in 1930, was opened by the then Minister of Labour (Margaret Bondfield) and received widespread publicity. A much-prized order from Claridges followed (see page 102) and, when it was completed, one Welsh and one Durham quilter were invited to London for the day as the guests of the hotel management. Mrs Amy Thomas of Aberdare represented Wales and her impressions of the day are recorded in *Rural Industries*, the magazine of the RIB:

To my delight I gazed upon a few specimens of our own handiwork, little had I dreamed that our quilts would ever occupy such a place. What pleased me most was to discover the wonderful blending in design and colour of the quilts with the tone of the decorations of the rooms . . . It pleased me also to find that the quilts made at Aberdare Centre maintained a standard of efficiency in design and workmanship equal to those made at the other Centres.[10]

The Abertridwr class   The organization of the Abertridwr class is well remembered by two RIB quilters still living in the area who both joined as young girls in the early 1930s. Twenty started in the class. They met first in the Wesleyan Chapel, then the treasurer's house, but moved from home to home as numbers dwindled, through to the Second World War. Their teacher was Miss Owen, whose family came from Porth and whose mother had been a quilter. She was a hard task master, insisting on high-quality work and encouraging experimentation.

The class was taught for 16 weeks, during which time the teacher was paid, but pupils made trial quilts without pay. After that, the group continued alone, making quilts to order: prices charged for the most expensive quilts (silk ones) are shown in fig. 87. Orders came regularly both via the Rural Industries Bureau and from wealthy Cardiff families. Fabrics were supplied with the orders, but the class provided thread and wool for wadding. Bought by the sackful, the wool had first to be soaked, washed with soap powder to clean it and remove the oil, then dried and carded for use. One person was usually given the job of preparing the wool for the group whilst the others quilted.

The techniques used were based on traditional Welsh practice. Quilts were pinned into the frame with only the 'mid point and quarters' marked, *then* the designs were marked out using tailor's chalk broken into points. Frames were set upon trestles and four quilters worked either side of a frame. Overalls were worn as they worked and an unfinished quilt was always covered with a cloth at the end of a working day to keep it clean. The quilters worked most weekday mornings and could finish a cot quilt in a couple of days, but a closely worked double-bed sized quilt might take two to three weeks.

The Abertridwr group continued right through the 1930s but numbers fell through the decade as the younger women married. By the outbreak of war in 1939 only two were left and, though one continued to work for her own pleasure, the RIB scheme had come to an end and no longer provided any orders.

Post-war years   Although the RIB scheme ended in 1939, it left a longer legacy in Wales than in Durham. More quilters had been involved in a smaller area and when a number of former teachers and quilters began to teach at Adult Education classes, in the post-war period, they found a steady demand.

In 1951, the Welsh Folk Museum organized a conference on quilting, together with a quiltmaking competition, won by Miss Emiah Jones of Crossheads, Carmarthenshire, with the beautiful quilt in fig. 88. Nothing about this quilt is distinctively Welsh; instead it has Miss Jones's own individual stamp – her use of very close quilting to create a stippled effect. It was a technique both she and her pupils used to good effect and is reminiscent of a similar

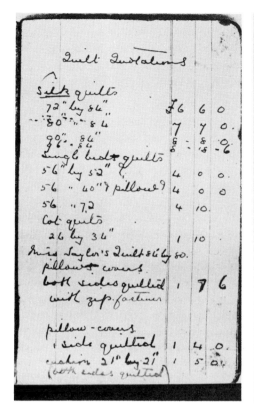

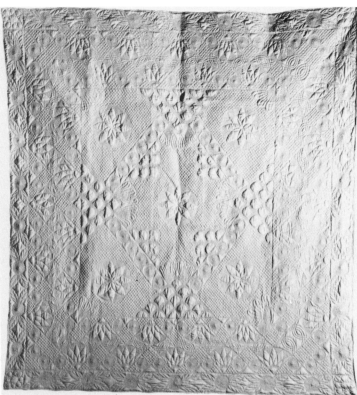

style of quilting on a West Country quilt made a century and a half beforehand.[11] The Welsh Folk Museum conference was intended to stimulate renewed quiltmaking activity. But times had changed. With the prosperity and mobility of post-war Britain, there was no longer a desperate need to earn a living at a quilting frame. Women increasingly sought both work and pleasure outside the home. Adult Education classes in quilting did continue for some years (Kate Lewis continued teaching until the mid-1960s), but produced mainly small items (cushions, tea cosies or cot quilts) – pieces which never seem quite to achieve the quality and beauty of a large bed quilt. In more recent years, these have been replaced by classes and informal groups whose quiltmaking activities are less locally influenced but, instead, draw upon more broadly based traditional and contemporary influences.

Characteristics of Welsh quilts

As in the North of England, certain patterns and the manner in which they are used are generally recognized as characteristic of Welsh quilts. The regional style evolved probably in the first half of the nineteenth century and carried through into the twentieth century with little basic change, until the RIB scheme of the 1930s.

Welsh quilters, especially those in rural areas, used fewer templates than those in the North of England. Many patterns were drawn using a ruler or a piece of chalk on the end of a string. The use of geometrically divided borders, overlapping circles and half-circles were, therefore, particularly common, for these could be drawn with this very basic equipment. The appearance of a particular pattern associated with the Welsh tradition on a quilt is no guarantee that it is a Welsh quilt – only an indication that it might be! The overall style and use of pattern must be looked at as closely as the individual pattern elements themselves.

87. Abertridwr quilt prices from class accounts book

88. Wholecloth quilt quilted with a bordered quilting design. Made by Miss Emiah Jones of Banc-y-ffynon, Glamorgan and awarded first prize at the Welsh Folk Museum exhibition of quilting: 1951

Allover designs and filling patterns   The simple *allover* patterns used throughout Britain (*square-diamonds*, *shell*, *wineglass* and *wave*) were used in Welsh quilts too. But two patterns: (1) *sea waves* (fig. 31e); and (2) a large-scale variant of the *plate* patterns (in which the overlapping circles are filled with veins to produce the characteristic Welsh *beech-leaf* – fig. 14a) are typically Welsh. Both patterns are based on circles and could be simply drawn with the 'chalk and string' technique.

Bordered designs   Welsh *bordered* designs have, for the most part, retained the long-established characteristic of having the borders, central motif and corner motifs contained within lines of quilting. It is this characteristic which distinguishes them from some North Country quilts and has led Welsh quilts to be described as 'geometric' in style. But it is an old style of quilting design which is also found on most North Country and West Country quilts from the first half of the nineteenth century. Typically Welsh motifs used within *bordered* designs include *beech-leaf*, *bent-leaf*, *spiral* or *snail-creep*, *paisley* '*pear*', *heart*, *tudor-rose* and *tulip* (figs. 17, 18 and 23). Some are not uncommon outside Wales: *hearts* for example, are a characteristic of marriage quilts from any region, and a slimmer version of *tulip* is used on North Country quilts. A form of *spiral* pattern is also found on North Country quilts in the 'Gardiner style' but here they are less formally used than on Welsh quilts and are more open in outline.

Typical border patterns are often geometric with diagonal lines dividing the border into squares and triangles. Fig. 82 shows these clearly drawn on a quilt top. Another characteristically Welsh border is *church-window*, based on overlapping semi-circles which, again, could be drawn with chalk and string. The spaces left by the geometric divisions could be filled in whatever way the quilter chose. When linked motifs were used as a border pattern the usual Welsh choice was a *spiral* or *crested wave*. *Cable twist* and *twist* borders were also used.

The fabrics and general style can identify a Welsh origin. Welsh quilters liked strong colours and used them in a bold fashion, especially on wool quilts. Everyday quilts from Wales tend to be thicker and heavier than their North Country counterparts; stitches were, therefore, larger and often in a dark-coloured linen thread. But the thicker padding, combined with the geometric style of design, could produce a more sculptured look – one of the particularly attractive characteristics of Welsh quilts.

9 Scottish Quilts

We made haaps ti mak use o' the worn blaankets –
ye couldna' throw them oot. They'd last aboot
fifty years like this.
Daisy Aitchison, former herring girl
from Eyemouth (1985)[1]

Scotland has always had a tradition of fine needlework but, so far, little evidence of a quilting tradition. Patchwork coverlets in mosaic, crazy and log-cabin patterns, in typical Victorian style, were made in much of Scotland, even as far as the Northern Isles. Patchwork coverlets embroidered with bible texts were worked in those communities with a strong religious element. But of traditional *quilts* there has so far been little trace and no known record. This had always seemed curious. Traditional quilts had been made throughout Northumberland in the nineteenth century. Such close cultural and geographical links existed between Northumberland and the Scottish Borders, it was difficult to understand how quiltmaking could stop at the Border. It seems that it did not.

Despite the lack of evidence for a Scottish quiltmaking tradition, ornate and perhaps professionally made quilts were as much in evidence in the castles and country homes of Scotland as they were elsewhere in Britain. A handful of seventeenth- and eighteenth-century examples have survived, typical of their age and genre, but their precise origin is unknown.

The oldest surviving traditional-style quilts known to have been made in Scotland are illustrated in figs. 89 and 90. The quilt in fig. 89 is a medallion quilt of red and white printed cottons, roughly quilted in an allover *wave* pattern. It was made by Nicholas White, a native of Dundee, who worked as a whaling ship steward. He died in 1897 at the age of 53 but when he made the quilt is not known. The quilt is pieced from over a hundred different prints, all in red and white, so the possibility arises that Nicholas White had access to the sample books produced by textile factories in the Vale of Leven, which manufactured Turkey Red prints. An upsurge of textile production took place there in the 1870s and 1880s following the invention of the alazarin form of the Turkey Red dye. The water in that area was particularly suited to the chemical dyeing process.

How did Nicholas White come to make this medallion quilt? Was the design as common in Scotland as elsewhere in Britain? It is a unique example from Scotland, but almost certainly owes its survival to its whaling connections rather than to its intrinsic quality as a quilt. Were other medallion quilts made which no one saw fit to preserve? Tantalizing questions to which there are as yet no answers.

A detail of the other quilt, made around 1860, is shown in fig. 90. This wholecloth quilt of cotton sateen, pink on one side and light beige on the other, was made by Mrs Johnston, a blacksmith's wife, who lived near St Andrews in Fifeshire.[2] So far it appears unique. Was it one of many wholecloth quilts – its existence only brought to light by chance? Or does it represent an outside influence, perhaps from migrating mining families from the North of England?

89. *Medallion quilt in red and white cotton prints and quilted with an allover wave pattern. Made by Nicholas White of Dundee (1844–97), a whaling ship steward (240 × 230 cm—95 × 90 in.)*

It does seem that the survival of so few traditional quilts confirms that the tradition of quiltmaking was never widespread in Scotland. The role of quilts as bed covers in other parts of Britain was filled in Scotland by woven woollen blankets and coverlets, and by wool rugs. But in southern parts – in the Borders and possibly in Galloway too – quiltmaking did become quite widespread in the nineteenth century, with strong links to the patterns and techniques of North Country quilts. Older women in the farming districts and towns of the Borders, and in east coast fishing villages, remember past generations of their families making quilts. The strongest visual memory is of quilt frames, either in use or stored in the house; few informants could give much detail of the quilts made and patterns used.

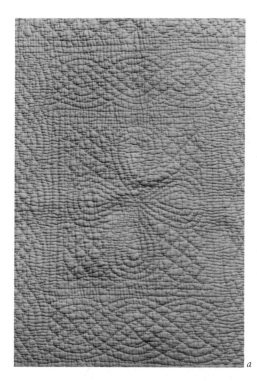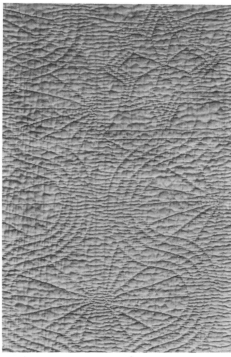

a *b*

*90. Centre (a), corner
and border detail (b)
of wholecloth quilt
quilted with a
bordered quilting
design. Made by Mrs
Johnston of Fifeshire:
c.1860*

A handful of quilts made in these areas have survived in families. All are wholecloth quilts, quilted either in simple *strip* designs or *bordered* designs strongly influenced by the North Country tradition of the late nineteenth century. Though very utilitarian, two quilts contain border patterns not seen elsewhere (fig. 91). The *cable-twist* variation is from an all-white wholecloth cotton quilt. But the *rope* pattern is from a quilt made by a former herring girl from the fishing village of Eyemouth, now in her eighties. One of three quilts she made before she was married, this one was covered with purple sateen – 'Italian Cloth' she called it, bought in Berwick. These blanket-filled quilts were called *haps* (pronounced 'haap' in Scotland), a term used for wool quilts in Northumberland and a shortened version of the word *happin* or *happen* used throughout Scotland and much of northern England for centuries to mean a warm covering of some kind.

All three of these *haps* for the *kist* – the Scottish equivalent of a 'bottom drawer' – were made in the late 1920s. It was the custom for worn blankets to be re-used in this way, not for top bed covers, but to be used as blanket substitutes under an all-white coverlet. 'Everyone had white counterpanes, ye ken.' They were made by their owner in her spare time when she worked as a herring gutter. 'that was nae joke; ye jest had to tak that when ye could get a chance for sewing. Winter time ye got a better chance for i' the summer time ye worked fra six o'clock i' the mornin ti twelve a' night guttin fish.'[3]

Not only the young girls of Eyemouth made quilts, but professional quilters, too, worked in the village. In the 1920s and 1930s Isabella Black, whose husband was a cooper, made quilts for villagers to give as wedding presents for family and friends. She charged 14s (70p) but what kind of quilt she made for such a small sum is not known. The quilt in fig. 92 was also made for a wedding present at a much later date (1960s) by a quilter still living in Eyemouth. Another quilter in the village charged £3 for quilts which took two weeks to make (1920s). But her wholecloth quilts were closely quilted, 'North Country style', for she

91. Border patterns traced from early twentieth century quilts from the Scottish borders: (a) rope; (b) cable twist *variation*

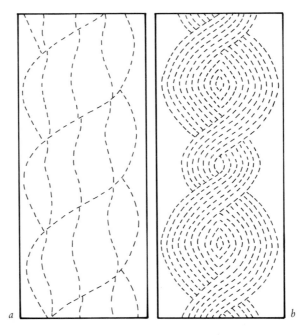

92. Wholecloth quilt in blue cotton sateen (reverse, cream) quilted with a bordered *quilting design. Made by Ailsa Dougall of Eyemouth, Borders Region, to a pattern belonging to her grandmother: 1963 (216 × 204 cm—84 × 80 in.)*

had been apprenticed to a quilter in Belford, Northumberland.[4]

In another part of the Scottish Borders, a different quiltmaking tradition emerged. In the districts around Melrose a type of 'eiderdown' was made by tightly stuffing a muslin case, stitched into large sections, with cleaned and carded wool. The muslin case was then covered with fabric to choice. One lady, Mabel Preston, still makes 'quilts' like this – she learned from her mother, who in turn, learned from an elderly local lady from a group of itinerant quilters.

Though a splendid example of adapting locally available materials to produce a useful and (then) fashionable article, the social traditions of this type of quiltmaking are especially interesting for the way in which they parallel traditional hand-stitched quilting. Quilting parties were a regular part of social life in this Border area. 'We went to quilting parties at night because everyone worked in the day. They were lovely times.'[5] Whilst work progressed, the ladies entertained themselves by reciting dialect poems of which Mrs Preston still has an extensive repertoire. Itinerant quilters also travelled in small groups around the Border homes of the gentry, making these stuffed quilts for the household.

Quilting in Scotland has received so little attention it is hard to relate what now survives and is remembered to a period beyond living memory. Certainly no distinct regional quilting tradition evolved in the country as a whole and, indeed, in the Gaelic culture of the Highlands and Islands, making wadded quilts apparently had no place. But in Lowland Scotland, especially in the Borders, quilting was practised where links with English counties along the Border were close. Perhaps future research will uncover more and help to paint a more complete picture of the role of traditional quilting in Scotland.

93. Wholecloth quilt in cotton sateen discovered in Scotland. The style of the bordered quilting design suggests it is a 'stamped' quilt marked by a quilt designer from Allendale or Weardale, probably for a Scottish customer

Appendix: Selected References to Quilts in Wills, Household Inventories and Accounts (1400–1800)

FIFTEENTH CENTURY

1454   *Durham Account Rolls*: 'ij qwhiltez . . . j whilte'[a]

1476   Will of John Trollop, of Thornley, Co. Durham: 'unam mappam de Twild'[b]

1477   *Ripon Chapter Acts*: 'unum twylt'[a]

SIXTEENTH CENTURY

1540   Twenty-three quilts of sarsenet given to Katherine Howard from the Royal Wardrobe[c]

1551   From an inventory of Edward, last feudal baron of Powys, Powys Castle, Montgomery:
'*In the New Chamber over ye Garden* . . . Item a qwylte of red silk
In the Nursery . . . Item, a fether bed, a bowater, a qwylte, and a coverlet of dornes'[d]

1557   Inventory of Jane Lawson, Nesham: '*In the Chamber ouer the Hall* . . . A quilt and iiij blankets . . . and a happinge'[b]

1560   Will of Dame Joyce Carye, Thremhall: 'To . . . my son . . . a quilt of blue sarcenet, a coverlet of arras work, 2 of my best featherbeds, a pair of fustian blankets, 2 pair of fine sheets, 2 pair of pillowberes . . .'[e]

1562   Household schedule of John de Veer, 16th Earl of Oxford, Lord Great Chamberlain of England: 'One quilt of red sarcenet'[j]

1566   Inventory of William Walton of Durham, draper: 'A covering wrought of silk . . . a twilt, a happing'[b]

1577   Inventory of Leonard Temperley, Witton Gilbert, Co. Durham: 'j quilte . . . and olde happin harden'[b]

1578   Will of Lady Phillipa Smith, of Hill Hall:
'*To my sister Copland* . . . in the Great Chamber a quilt of red, green and yellow damask . . .
To my neice Barratt . . . a quilt of red, blue and green damask . . .
To my cousin Jane Lucas . . . in my chamber a home-made coverlet . . . a quilt of green sarcenet'[e]

1583   Will of Thomas, Earl of Sussex: 'To Sir Henry [brother] . . . a standing bed of purple satin embroidered with lozenges of cloth of silver and gold with curtains and quilt, a standing bed of green velvet and cloth of silver with curtains and quilt, a standing bed of crimson bodkin and tawny velvet with stars and Stafford knots with curtains and quilt of red and yellow sarcenet . . . a quilt of red and yellow silk like birds' eyes . . . a quilt of red silk like to birds' eyes . . . the quilts, chairs, stools, cushions . . . which was (*sic*) in her Majesty's Withdrawing Chamber.'[e]

1584   Inventory of Robert Dudley, Earl of Leicester: 'A faire quilte of crymson sattin, vi breadths iij yards 3 quarters naile deep, all lozenged over with silver twiste, in the midst a cinquefoil with a garland of ragged staves, fringed aboute with a small fringe of crymson silk, lined through with white fustian.'[c]

1584   Inventory of John Stapleton, Llanbrynmair, Montgomery, '*In the P'rlor* . . . vj quiltinges'[d]

1592   Inventory of Sir John Perrot, Carew Castle, Pembrokeshire, 'Item ij old quiltes of yellowe sercnet, xx s. . . . Item a changeable silke quilt, price xx s. . . . Item an old black and white silke quilt for a bedd, price iiij s.'[d]

1594   Will of George Wilmer, Esquire, of West Ham, 'a quilt of taffeta'[e]

1597　Will of Dame Mary Judd, widow of
Sir Andrew Judd:
'*To my son* (in law) . . . my quilt of
purple taffeta . . .
To my daughter Golding . . . a quilt of
yellow and blue sarcenet'[e]

SEVENTEENTH CENTURY

1603　Inventory of Sir Thomas Kyston,
Hengrave, 'One twilt of tawny taffata
sarsenett embroydered all over w[th]
twiste of yellow silk, wth the
escutcheons of Sir Thomas Kyston's
and my ladye's armes'[c]

1609　Wardrobe accounts of James I, on the
occasion of the marriage of his
daughter the Princess Elizabeth: 'Item.
To John Baker, our upholsterer, for 3
quilts of fustian lined with taffeta, filled
with wool, and sewed with silk'[c]

1614　Inventory of Henry Howard, Earl of
Northampton: 'a china quilt stiched in
chequer worke with yealowe silke the
ground white'[c]

1619　Inventory of Robert Kefford, Sandy:
'On fetherbed, j bolster, j blankett, an
old quilt, 40 s.'[f]

1619　Inventory of Thomas Stacie,
gentleman, Hatley Port: '*In the chamber*
. . . six blanketts, one coverlet, one
quilt & a pair of curtains & valance'[f]

1619　Inventory of William Mason, tailor, St
John, Bedford: '*In a upper chamber* . . .
one old broken quilt 12d. . . . one
coverlet 13s 4d'[f]

1632　Inventory of Henry Percy, Earl of
Northumberland:
In the Redd Bedchamber . . . one olde
hollande quilt
In the Greene Bedd Chamber . . . one
holland quilt
In His Lordship's Chamber . . . one
crimson taffita quilt . . . one holland
quilt'[g]

1683　Inventory of the contents of
Wynnstay:
'*Over ye old parlor & passages* . . . 1
quilt bed and matt
Over the drawing roome . . . 1 quilt bed
and matt
Over the butry and hall . . . 1 quilt bed
The old parlor . . . 1 new quilt bed and
one old one

In ye Roome over ye last menconed roome
. . . 1 quilt bed'[d]

1689　Expense Book of John Hervey, first
Earl of Bristol: 'Paid Mary Bishop for
ye use and by order of Mrs Jane
Harrison for an India quilt for a bed,
£38'[c]

1689/　Inventory of William Garrat,
1690　gentleman, Writtle: '*In the hall chamber*
. . . one old quelt'[h]

1691　Inventory of William Bird, Horsely
Park, Writtle:
'*In the Pantry Chamber* . . . a gray
searge quilt
In the Parlor Chamber . . . a painted
callicoe quilt'[h]

EIGHTEENTH CENTURY

1700　Inventory of William Hills,
upholsterer, Newcastle upon Tyne: '1
quilt 0:5:0, 1 paire of blankets 0:2:0 . . .
1 rugg 0:1:6'[i]

1700　Inventory of Jane Hankin, widow,
Newcastle upon Tyne: 'two pair of
curtains and quilt 03:10:00 . . . one
craddle quilt 00:02:06'[i]

1705　Inventory of Zachariah Day,
blacksmith, Roxwell: '*In the Parlor* . . .
a quilt'[h]

1705　Inventory of Elizabeth Eree, widow,
Writtle: '*In the Chamber over the Parlour*
. . . one quilt'[h]

1710　Inventory of William Wogan,
Llanstinan, Pembrokeshire: '*Room over
Cedar Room* . . . old quilt
Oak Room . . . quilt
Great Parlour . . . quilt with pillows'[d]

1711　Inventory of the contents of 'The
Yellow Nursery' (in *The Russells of
Bloomsbury*): 'one Tristram quilt, 3
blankets and a calico quilt'[d]

1719　Inventory of John Overill, miller,
Roxwell: '*In the Best Chamber* . . . one
quilt'[h]

1721　Account book entry (in *The Russells of
Bloomsbury*): 'May 1, 1721. Paid Mrs
Putts Her Grace's share of a raffle for a
quilt at Southampton House per order
£3. 3s. od.'[d]

1723　Inventory of John Herridge, yeoman,
Writtle: '*In the Great Parlour* . . . one
quilt'[h]

1729   Inventory of Margaret Haward, widow, Writtle: '*In the Parlor* . . . one quilt' (listed with bedstedle, vallance, curtains, curtain rods and three blankets to a total value of £3)[h]

1771   Inventory (in *The Russells of Bloomsbury*) includes: '*Her Grace's Bed Chamber* . . . a counterpane same as bed lined with tammy; a small white silk quilt'[d]

1786   In the *Bristol Journal* of Sarah Farley, an entry for 4 Feb. 1786 mentions 'All the Household furniture' including 'Blankets, Quilts and cotton Counterpanes'[d]

SOURCES

(Full details of these references are given in the Bibliography, page 163.)

[a] *Oxford English Dictionary*
[b] Surtees Society (1835)
[c] Colby (1972)
[d] Fitzrandolph (1954)
[e] Emmison (1978)
[f] Emmison (1938)
[g] Batho (1962)
[h] Steer (1950)
[i] Department of Palaeography, University of Durham
[j] Emmison (1980)

Notes

Full details of the references cited are given in the Bibliography, page oo.

Introduction

1. *Rural Industries*, Autumn 1931, p. 7.
2. Harrison, 1984, p. 13.

Chapter 1

1. Tyne and Wear Museums Craft Records (TWMCR), Shipley Art Gallery, Gateshead (collected 1978).
2. Colby, 1972, p. 21.
3. Fitzrandolph, 1954, p. 83.
4. ibid., p. 87.
5. Scott, 1935, p. 1.
6. Fitzrandolph, 1954, pp. 92–3.
7. Hake, 1937, p. 10.
8. personal communication, Mrs Snaith, Northumberland.
9. personal communication, Mrs Bell, Northumberland.
10. Fitzrandolph, 1954, p. 59.
11. Hake, 1937, p. 10.

Chapter 2

1. Fitzrandolph, 1954, p. 109.
2. TWMCR.
3. ibid.
4. Garrad, 1979, p. 40.
5. TWMCR.
6. ibid.
7. ibid.
8. Colby, 1958, p. 96 and fig. 110.
9. ibid., p. 60.
10. Jekyll, 1904, p. 126.

11. Holstein, 1973, fig. 15.
12. Colby, 1958, fig. 115.
13. TWMCR.
14. Colby, 1958, p. 20.
15. TWMCR.
16. Colby, 1972, p. 87.

Chapter 3

1. Quoted in undated newspaper cutting, personal memorabilia, Mrs Ripley, Co. Durham.
2. Percival, 1923, p. 2.
3. Fitzrandolph, 1954, p. 120.
4. ibid., p. 132.
5. TWMCR.
6. ibid.
7. Fitzrandolph, 1954, p. 129.
8. Quilters' Guild Tape Archive.
9. Fitzrandolph, 1954, p. 124.
10. Colby, 1972, p. 87.
11. Swain, 1970, p. 36 and pl. 16.
12. Fitzrandolph, 1954, p. 124 and fig. 13.
13. Fitzrandolph and Fletcher, 1972, p. 12.
14. TWMCR.
15. Fitzrandolph, 1954, p. 79.

Chapter 4

1. TWMCR.
2. Fitzrandolph, 1954, p. 122.
3. personal communication, Mrs Hughes, Co. Durham.
4. Hake, 1937, p. 12.

5. TWMCR.
6. Fitzrandolph, 1954, p. 75.
7. Quilters' Guild Tape Archive.
8. TWMCR.
9. personal communication, Miss Watson, Co. Durham.
10. personal communication, Mrs Stirling, Sunderland.
11. personal communication, Mrs Bell, Northumberland.
12. TWMCR.
13. ibid.
14. personal communication, Mrs Emms, Co. Durham.
15. Hake, 1937, p. 15.
16. Jones, 1975, p. 7.
17. Fitzrandolph and Fletcher, 1972, p. 43.
18. ibid.
19. TWMCR.

Chapter 5

1. Colby, 1972, p. 1.
2. Peto, 1949, p. 7.
3. Hake, 1937, p. 1.
4. Harrison, 1984, p. 13.
5. Barley, 1961, p. xviii.
6. Symons and Preece, 1928, pl. iv (1 and 2); pl. x (2); pl ix (1); pl. viii (2).
7. ibid., p. 83.
8. Colby, 1972, p. 8.
9. Wright, 1962, p. 36.
10. Colby, 1972, p. 18.
11. Fitzrandolph, 1954, p. 156.
12. Colby, 1972, p. 90.
13. Fitzrandolph, 1954, p. 153.

14. *Oxford English Dictionary*: quilting.
15. Colby, 1972, p. 83.
16. Bennett, 1956, p. 83.
17. Hoskins, 1957, p. 295.
18. Quoted in Hoskins, 1957, p. 119.
19. Hoskins, 1957, p. 295.
20. Colby, 1972, p. 21.
21. ibid., p. 99.
22. ibid., fig. 105.
23. Victoria and Albert Museum, 1949, pl. 1.
24. Colby, 1972, p. 102.
25. Parker, 1984, p. 97.
26. Irwin and Brett, 1970, p. 3.
27. ibid., p. 4.
28. ibid.
29. ibid., pl. 11.
30. Percival, 1923, p. 20.
31. Emmison, 1938, 22/3/1619.
32. Steer, 1950, 30/1/1689.
33. ibid., 26/5/1691.
34. Colby, 1972, p. 41.
35. ibid., p. 42.
36. Defoe, 1724–6, vol. 1, p. 82.
37. Buck, 1979, p. 65.
38. ibid., p. 198.
39. Steer, 1950, 19/5/1730.
40. Wills and inventories for 1700, Department of Palaeography, University of Durham.
41. Steer, 1950, 26/5/1691.
42. Colby, 1958, p. 96.
43. TWMCR.
44. Fitzrandolph, 1954, p. 45.
45. Lee, 1950, p. 43.
46. Fitzrandolph, 1954, p. 45.
47. Wilson, 1872, p. 57.
48. personal communication, Mrs Snaith, Northumberland.
49. TWMCR.
50. Report of work of RIB, 1929–36.
51. RIB report for year ending 30/9/1928.
52. Letter to author, Angela Brocklebank, 6/6/1985.
53. *Rural Industries*, Summer 1932.

Chapter 6
1. TWMCR.
2. Allgood Papers, ZAL 81/24, Northumberland Record Office.
3. Hake Papers, letter from A. M. Auchinvole, December 1937.
4. ibid., unpublished article by Mavis Fitzrandolph, 24/8/1936.
5. ibid., letter from C. C. Brown, undated (*c*.1939).
6. Hake, 1937, p. 6.
7. Letter to author, Margaret King, 7/8/1985.
8. Fitzrandolph, 1954, p. 31.
9. Jones, 1975, p. 5.
10. Colby, 1972, p. 142.
11. Lee, 1950, p. 212–13.
12. Quoted in Wilson, 1872, p. 10.
13. TWMCR.
14. Quilters' Guild Tape Archive.
15. personal communication, Miss Shepherd, Northumberland.

Chapter 7
1. TWMCR.
2. Surtees Society, 1874.
3. Surtees Society, 1835.
4. TWMCR.
5. Morris, 1982, p. 175.
6. Colby, 1958, fig. 110.
7. Newcastle City Library, undated.
8. *North Country Lore and Legend*, 1887, p. 224.
9. Garrad, 1979, p. 41.
10. personal communication, John Gall, Beamish Museum.
11. personal communication, Mrs Ripley, Co. Durham.
12. Fitzrandolph, 1954, p. 40.
13. ibid., p. 43.

14. ibid.
15. ibid.
16. personal communication, Mrs Hope, Northumberland.
17. TWMCR.
18. personal communication, Joanna Hashagen, Bowes Museum.
19. TWMCR.
20. Hake, 1937, p. 7.
21. Hake Papers, note by Mavis Fitzrandolph.
22. Hake, 1937, p. 7.
23. ibid., p. 3.
24. ibid., p. 5.
25. ibid., p. 4.
26. ibid., p. 3.
27. Hake Papers, letter from Miss Stamp.
28. ibid.
29. Hake, 1937, p. 3.
30. *Oxford English Dictionary*: quilt.

Chapter 8
1. Fitzrandolph, 1954, p. 28.
2. Anthony, 1972, p. 36.
3. Fitzrandolph, 1954, p. 28.
4. ibid., p. 93.
5. ibid., p. 94.
6. personal communication, Mrs Williams, Sunderland.
7. Fitzrandolph, 1937, p. 34.
8. ibid., p. 45.
9. ibid., p. 50.
10. *Rural Industries*, Autumn 1932, p. 4.
11. Hake, 1937, fig. 36.

Chapter 9
1. personal communication, Mrs Aitchison, Eyemouth.
2. personal communication, Mrs Spoors, Newcastle upon Tyne.
3. personal communication, Mrs Aitchison.
4. personal communication, Mrs Rosie, Eyemouth.
5. *Scotsman*, April 1982.

Bibliography

ANSCOMBE, I. (1984): *A Woman's Touch: Women in Design from 1860 to the Present Day.* Virago, London.

ANTHONY, I. E. (1972): 'Quilting and Patchwork in Wales', *Amgueddfa*, 1972, pp. 2–15.

BARLEY, M. W. (1961): *The English Farmhouse and Cottage.* Routledge and Kegan Paul, London.

BATHO, G. R. (1962): *The Household Papers of Henry Percy, Ninth Earl of Northumberland, 1564–1632.* Royal Historical Society, London.

BATSFORD, H. and FRY, C. (1938): *The English Cottage.* B. T. Batsford, London.

BENNETT, H. S. (1956): *Life on the English Manor: A Study of Peasant Conditions, 1150–1400.* Cambridge University Press, Cambridge.

BOWES MUSEUM (1985): *A Selection of Twenty Quilt and Patchwork Bedcovers.* Bowes Museum, Barnard Castle.

BUCK, A. (1979): *Dress in Eighteenth-Century England.* B. T. Batsford, London.

BURNETT, J. (1977): *Useful Toil: Autobiographies of Working People from the 1820s–1920s.* Penguin, Harmondsworth.

CHAPLIN, S. (1978): 'Durham Mining Villages', in BULMER, M. (ed.): *Mining and Social Change.* Croom Helm, London.

COLBY, A. (1958) *Patchwork.* B. T. Batsford, London.

COLBY, A. (1972) *Quilting.* B. T. Batsford, London.

DAVIES, S. (1963) *North Country Bred: A Working Class Family Chronicle.* Routledge and Kegan Paul, London.

DEFOE, D. (1724–6) *A Tour through England and Wales*, 2 vols. Reprinted 1928, Dent, London.

DIXON, H. (1974) *An Allendale Miscellany.* Frank Graham, Newcastle.

DURHAM COUNTY FEDERATION OF WOMEN'S INSTITUTES (undated): *Durham Quilting.* DCFWI, Durham.

EMMISON, F. G. (1938): 'Jacobean Household Inventories', *Publications of Bedfordshire Historical Society*, vol. 20.

EMMISON, F. G. (1978): *Elizabethan Life: Wills of Essex Gentry and Merchants.* Essex Record Office, Chelmsford.

EMMISON, F. G. (1980): *Elizabethan Life: Wills of Essex Gentry and Yeomen.* Essex Record Office, Chelmsford.

FITZRANDOLPH, M. (1954): *Traditional Quilting.* B. T. Batsford, London.

FITZRANDOLPH, M. and FLETCHER, F. M. (1972): *Quilting.* Dryad Press, Leicester.

GARRAD, L. S. (1979): 'Quilting and Patchwork in the Isle of Man', *Folk Life*, vol. 17, pp. 39–48.

HAKE, E. (1937): *English Quilting Old and New.* B. T. Batsford, London.

HARRISON, J. F. C. (1984): *The Common People.* Fontana, London.

HILL, C. P. (1977): *British Economic and Social History, 1700–1975.* Edward Arnold, London.

HOLSTEIN, J. (1973): *The Pieced Quilt: An American Design Tradition.* New York Graphic Society, Little Brown & Co., Boston.

HOSKINS, W. G. (1957): *The Midland Peasant: The Economic and Social History of a Leicestershire Village.* Macmillan, London.

IRWIN, J. and BRETT, K. B. (1970): *Origins of Chintz.* HMSO, London.

JEKYLL, G. (1904): *Old West Surrey.* Kohler and Coombes, London.

JONES, L. (1975): 'Quilting', *Ulster Folklife*, vol. 21, pp. 1–9.

JONES, L. (1978): 'Patchwork Bedcovers', *Ulster Folklife*, vol. 24, pp. 31–47.

JUSTEMA, W. (1976): *Pattern: A Historical Perspective*. Paul Elak, London.

LEE, J. (1950): *Weardale Memories and Traditions*. Published by author.

MONTGOMERY, F. M. (1970): *Printed Textiles: English and American Cottons and Linens, 1700–1850*. Thames and Hudson, London.

MORRIS, C. (ed.) (1982): *The Illustrated Journeys of Celia Fiennes, 1685–c.1712*. Macdonald & Co., London and Sydney.

NEWCASTLE CITY LIBRARY (undated): collected papers relating to the murder of Joseph Hedley. Local History Library, Newcastle upon Tyne.

North Country Lore and Legend (1887): 'Joe the Quilter', July, pp. 221–4.

PARKER, R. (1984): *The Subversive Stitch*. The Women's Press, London.

PERCIVAL, M. (1923): *The Chintz Book*. Heinemann, London.

PETO, F. (1939): *Historic Quilts*. American Historical Co. Inc., New York.

PETO, F. (1949): *American Quilts and Coverlets*. Max Parrish, London.

Rural Industries (various issues, 1928–36). Rural Industries Bureau, London.

SCOTT, B. (1935): *The Craft of Quilting*. Dryad Press, Leicester.

STEER, F. W. (ed.) (1950): *Farm and Cottage Inventories of Mid-Essex, 1635–1749*. Phillimore, London and Chichester.

SURTEES SOCIETY (1835): *Wills and Inventories*, Surtees Society, vol. 2.

SURTEES SOCIETY (1844): *Durham Household Book*. Surtees Society, vol. 18.

SURTEES SOCIETY (1874): *Ripon Chapter Acts*. Surtees Society, vol. 64.

SURTEES SOCIETY (1898): *Durham Account Rolls*. Surtees Society, vol. 99.

SWAIN, M. H. (1970): *Historical Needlework: A Study of Influences in Scotland and Northern England*. Barry and Jenkins, London.

SYMONS, M. and PREECE, L. (1928): *Needlework Through the Ages*. Hodder and Stoughton, London.

TOWNSEND, A. R. and TAYLOR, C. C. (1975): 'Regional Culture and Identity in Industrialized Societies: the Case of North East England', *Regional Studies*, vol. 9, pp. 379–93.

VICTORIA AND ALBERT MUSEUM (1949): *Notes on Quilting*. HMSO, London.

WARD, A. (1966): 'Quilting in the North of England', *Folk Life*, vol. 4, pp. 75–83.

WHEELER, R. F. (1885): *The Northumbrian Pitman: His Works and Ways*. Mawson, Swan and Morgan, Newcastle upon Tyne.

WILLIAMSON, W. (1982): *Class Culture and Community: A Biographical Study of Social Change in Mining*. Routledge and Kegan Paul, London.

WILSON, T. (1872): *The Pitman's Pay* (originally published 1843). Routledge, London.

WRIGHT, L. (1962): *Warm and Snug: The History of the Bed*. Routledge and Kegan Paul, London.

Practical books for quiltmaking (including patchwork and appliqué)

GOOD HOUSEKEEPING (1983): *Quilting and Patchwork*. Ebury Press, London.

JAMES, M. (1978): *The Quiltmaker's Handbook*. Prentice-Hall, Englewood Cliffs, NJ.

JAMES, M. (1981): *The Second Quiltmaker's Handbook*. Prentice-Hall, Englewood Cliffs, NJ.

WALKER, M. (1985): *Quiltmaking*. Ebury Press, London.

Useful Addresses

SUPPLIERS

Fabrics, sewing equipment, books etc.

UK

Patchwork Dog and the Calico Cat (shop and mail order)
21 Chalk Farm Road
London NW1

Pioneer Patches (mail order)
Inglewood Lodge
Birkby Road
Huddersfield
Yorkshire HD2 2DA

Quilter's Patch (shop and mail order)
82 Gillygate
York YO3 7EQ

Strawberry Fayre (mail order)
Chagford
Newton Abbot
Devon TQ13 8EN

Village Fabrics (shop and mail order)
40 Goldsmith's Lane
Wallingford
Oxfordshire

USA

For a fully comprehensive list covering all parts of the USA, see *The Quilter's Catalog: A Complete Guide to Quilting Sources and Supplies*, by Linda Stokes, Main Street Press, New Jersey.

Frames

Cyril Smith
49 Braemar Drive
Christchurch
Dorset BH23 5NN

Abbotsdene Crafts
76 Roman Road
Basingstoke
Hampshire RG23 8HB

Tollers Design Centre for Arts and Crafts
Tollers Farm
Drive Road
Old Coulsdon
Surrey CR3 1BN

Patterns

CoSIRA
141 Castle Street
Salisbury
Wiltshire SP1 3TP

Durham County Federation of Women's Institutes
51–2 Crossgates
Durham DH1 4PY

The Quiltery
Tacolneston
Norwich
Norfolk NR16 1DW

Books and magazines

UK

Craft Publications (needlework and craft book suppliers)
Unit 5C
5 West Hill
Aspley Guise
Milton Keynes MK17 8DP

Faith Legg (secondhand needlecraft books)
The Guildhall Bookroom
Church Street
Eye
Suffolk IP23 7BD

Judith Mansfield (secondhand needlecraft books)
60a Dornton Road
London SW12 9NE

Quilters' Guild Newsletter (quarterly)
Editorial Office
13 Woodgreen Road
Winchester
Hampshire SO22 6LH

Patchwork and Quilting (quarterly)
29 Broadlands Drive
Malvern
Worcestershire WR14 1PW
Tel: 06845 3966

USA and Canada

Quilters' Newsletter Magazine
6700 West 44th Avenue
Wheatridge
Colorado 80033
USA

The Professional Quilter
Oliver Press
1409B Farrington
St Paul
Minnesota 55117
USA

Quilt
PO Box 14373
North Palm Beach
Florida 33408
USA

Uncoverings
(Research Papers of the
American Quilt Study
Group)
105 Molino Avenue
Mill Valley
California 94941
USA

Canada Quilts
13 Pinewood Avenue
Grimsby
Ontario L3M 1WN
Canada

ORGANIZATIONS

Quilters' Guild
Secretary: Margaret Petit
56 Wilcot Road
Pewsey
Wiltshire SN9 5EC

Patchwork Guild of Northern
Ireland
c/o Deborah Baillie
288 Stranmillis Road
Belfast BT9 5D2

Irish Patchwork Society
Information Officer: Ann
McDermott
8 Raheen Green
off Blessington Road
Tallaght
County Dublin

MUSEUMS AND HISTORIC HOUSES

The Quilters' Guild has
compiled an extensive list of
quilts in museums and
historic houses which is
available on request (see
above for address of
secretary). Quilts in museums
are not always on open
display but in reference
collections. Access will be at
the discretion of museum
staff. The following museums
have particularly notable
collections of traditional
British quilts and/or sell
quilting publications and
slides.

BEAMISH: North of
England Open Air Museum
Beamish
Stanley
County Durham DH9 0RG

Bowes Museum
Barnard Castle
County Durham DL12 8NP

Gawthorpe Hall
Padiham
Burnley
Lancashire BB12 8UA

Victoria and Albert Museum
Cromwell Road
South Kensington
London SW7 2RC

Ulster Folk and Transport
Museum
Cultra
Hollywood
County Down BT18 0EU

The Castle Museum
Tower Street
York YO1 1RY

Somerset County Museum
Taunton Castle
Taunton
Somerset TA1 4AA

Hereford City Museum and
Art Gallery
Broad Street
Hereford HR1 2LP

Index